Do any of the following statements portray your spiritual relationship with your spouse?

- We can't talk about spiritual things
- We never pray together
- I feel uncomfortable about sharing
- When it comes to spiritual matters, we're not close

Be assured you are not alone. Dr. Donald R. Harvey notes that this situation exists in the best of Christian marriages. He also observes that although the desire is there, most of us lack the knowledge to change the situation.

In these pages, Dr. Harvey shows how to close the gap of spiritual distance in your marriage. *The Spiritually Intimate Marriage* will help you discover the blessings of sharing your spiritual self with your mate and growing closer in Christ — together.

BY Donald R. Harvey
The Drifting Marriage
When the One You Love Wants to Leave
The Spiritually Intimate Marriage

THE SPIRITUALLY INTIMATE MARRIAGE

DONALD R. HARVEY

Fleming H. Revell Company
Tarrytown, New York

Scripture quotations are from The New English Bible. Copyright © The Delegates of the Oxford University Press and the Syndics of the Cambridge University Press 1961, 1970. Reprinted by permission.

All names of persons whose stories are shared have been changed, as have their situations, in order that privacy may be protected.

Library of Congress Cataloging-in-Publication Data

Harvey, Donald R. (Donald Reid)
   The spiritually intimate marriage / Donald R. Harvey.
      p.   cm.
   ISBN 0-8007-5398-4
1. Marriage—Religious aspects—Christianity.   2. Spirituality.   3. Intimacy (Psychology)—Religious aspects—Christianity.   I. Title.
BV835.H377   1991
248.8'44—dc20   90-21354
                                                  CIP

Copyright © 1991 by Donald R. Harvey
Published by the Fleming H. Revell Company
Tarrytown, New York 10591
Printed in the United States of America

TO Jan,
whose constant love
has fostered in me
a desire to be
spiritually intimate

Contents

Part One   Coming to Grips 9

1   "I Don't Feel Close to You!" 11
2   "Are We the Only Ones Who Feel
        This Way?" 23
3   "What Is Spiritual Intimacy, Anyway?" 35
4   "Are There Prerequisites?" 49
5   "What Are the Benefits of Spiritual
        Intimacy?" 57

Part Two   Getting Started 59

6   The First Step: Assessing Your Level of
        Spiritual Intimacy 61
7   Turning the Corner: Choosing to
        Be Close 73
8   Developing Your Plan: Structuring Your
        Intimacy 83
9   What if Your Mate Isn't Ready? 95

Part Three   Dealing With the Interferences   105

10   "I Find It Uncomfortable to Share"   107
11   "I'm Not Spiritual Enough"   123
12   "Our Spiritual Differences Are
                    Divisive"   131
13   "We Don't Have the Time"   145
14   "How Do We Keep It Going?"   151

Conclusions   Is It Worth the Effort?   161

Appendix   Spiritual Intimacy in Marriage
                    Questionnaires   163

THE
SPIRITUALLY
INTIMATE
MARRIAGE

Part One
Coming to
Grips

1

"I Don't Feel Close to You!"

Marilyn's call came to me at my office. With the aid of a long-distance operator, she had tracked me down through information found on a book jacket. Even though hundreds of miles separated us geographically, there was no mistaking that Marilyn was a woman in severe emotional pain. Talking was a chore; her words came in short bursts instead of flowing easily; her tone of voice was tense.

> Dr. Harvey, my name is Marilyn. I know you don't know me, but I need to talk with someone. I feel like I'm stressed out, or burned out, or something. I just don't know anymore. All I do know is that I'm upset with the way my life is turning out.

Marilyn bypassed all of the usual courtesies: "Hello," "How are you?" "I hope things are going well." Instead, she got right to the point: she was in pain. Marilyn was an angry woman. In fact, she was as angry a person as I had talked with by phone. Her speech was so erratic and filled with emotion that it was difficult for me to a grasp what was really happening. I felt as if I were on a wild ride, hanging on for dear life. When faced with these situations, it is best to let people ventilate for a while. This usually results in a calmer disposition and a more productive conversation.

Marilyn continued to emote, and I continued to listen. She used words such as *confused* and *upset* fairly frequently. All along, I kept wondering what it was that had upset her so. As she began to calm down, Marilyn said something that started us moving in a clearer direction.

> I don't know if I've ever been this mad. I don't usually get upset—and never this upset. But sometimes, John makes me so mad.

Now we were getting somewhere. John was Marilyn's husband. I didn't know what he had done or not done. But it was clear that he figured in this somehow.

> Everyone thinks that my life has been just grand. "You're so fortunate, Marilyn." Maybe they're right. Sometimes I feel so guilty for being disappointed . . . for wanting things to be different. I just don't know what's right and what's wrong anymore.

I learned that Marilyn was the veteran of a thirty-year marriage. With the exception of two years when she and John were in seminary, their time together had been spent in ministry. John had pastored several churches during their married life, but from everything that Marilyn had to say, it appeared as though they had had three decades of success.

> John is a good man . . . and a spiritual man. It's not hard to see that. People have always loved him.

John was well liked in each of his pastorates, and his popularity always extended beyond the congregation. He was a true "credit to the church." This popularity was largely accredited to his desire to be active in civic affairs. John did not restrict his bent for service to just the church body. Rather, he felt a compassionate heart was also needed in the community at large. His attitude and behavior gained him the respect of a broad spectrum of people, but it also brought respect to the churches he pastored.

I couldn't help but feel warmly toward John. Marilyn described a compassionate man with a genuine heart for ministry. All of his churches experienced numerical growth. But even greater than that, people seemed to get grounded spiritually. "Churches were always strengthened." John was viewed as a spiritual man, not just a religious leader.

John's popularity always made moves a difficult matter. People loved him too much to want to let him go. There was never any dissension forcing them to look for another church. Instead, times of transition were always preceded by a sense that it was time to leave, that their work was nearing completion . . . that the Lord was leading them to another place of service.

All of their moves had been "good" moves. At least, good from a matter-of-fact career assessment. Each move had been a step up in congregational size. Their present church was no exception. It was viewed as the mother church of the region, and John now had the attention and respect of significant denominational leaders. I guess you could say that his ministry and career were going well.

> I never had any complaint with John's choice to enter the ministry. In fact, I have always enjoyed my role as a pastor's wife. He worked hard at pastoring, but I haven't been jealous of that. I've heard other wives describe their husbands' careers as mistresses, but I've never had those feelings toward John's ministry.

John's decision to enter the ministry came as no surprise to Marilyn. They had discussed his plans many times at great length before they married. In fact, rather than a negative, Marilyn viewed John's desire to enter the pastorate as a positive. It was an opportunity for her to also be of service. As they would move from church to church, Marilyn would quickly find her niche, filling in where needed. Not begrudgingly, but willingly, Marilyn would become John's primary support.

So far, so good. Marilyn's description of John was close to admirable. And whatever it was that prompted her anger, it did not seem to be either his career choice or the complicating consequences that naturally and frequently accompanied such a decision. Marilyn wasn't jealous of John's focus on ministry or the time demands. Neither was she upset about ministry transitions—the predictable times of "starting over" predicated by choosing to be in ministry. All of these things seemed to be pluses. But where were the negatives? What was it that had angered her so?

"Marilyn, thus far you've done a pretty good job of describing the things that you *aren't* mad about, but you've said nothing about what you *are* mad about. Exactly why are you mad at John?"

> I'm worried about our girls. Really, I'm concerned about the life-styles they're living. I tried to talk to John about it. As long as we were talking, that was okay. But when I suggested we pray about them, he just tuned me out. Boy, that made me mad!

John and Marilyn had raised three daughters in what appeared to be a stable Christian home. All three were now adults and living on their own. However, none were living what would be described as Christian life-styles. Marilyn was concerned about this and took it to John. But for some reason, he ignored her request to pray together. This incensed her.

Marilyn said that she was angry because of John's rebuff. Yet, I couldn't help but believe there was actually more to it than that. Marilyn's anger was too intense. At least, it seemed too intense to be caused by this incident alone. I'm not saying that John's rejection wouldn't have prompted a legitimate response of some kind. But Marilyn's anger was overwhelming. Few occurrences, in and of themselves, warrant such a reaction, and John's rejection did not qualify as one of these occurrences. Intensity of this magnitude usually suggests something historical. This could have either been in Marilyn's *personal history* or in her *marital history*; I wasn't sure which. But of one thing I was sure: There had to be more to it than just the current incident.

We bring a lot of baggage with us from childhood into adulthood. It's only natural. None of us came from perfect families. And even when home was good, that didn't exempt us from the unpredictables of life: deaths, traumatic events, geographical moves, peers, and so forth. There's a lot that can affect us as we grow up—a lot that makes up our personal history.

Probably most of what we face as children gets dealt with then. We make healthy adjustments and the experiences don't follow us around. At other times, however, these problems don't get satisfactorily settled. They don't get "resolved." It may have been child neglect or abuse, or possibly a home characterized by nonnurturing relationships or unpredictable and chaotic behavior. The possibilities are extensive, as are the consequences. Children who fail to resolve these experiences often enter adulthood with basic insecurities. This part of our personal history, which we inadvertently carry with us into adulthood, can then get in the way of our living healthy and productive lives.

With personal-history issues, it is the unsettled past that underlies the intensity of our reaction, not the present circumstance alone. Did Marilyn fall into this grouping? Were unresolved childhood issues fueling her intensity? Possibly. But at this point, I didn't have enough information to either rule this in or rule it out.

There was another possibility. Marilyn and John may have some unresolved issues within their relationship. Unresolved issues of a marital history are quite a bit different from those represented by an individual's personal history. One of the greatest differences is when and where these issues are developed. Personal issues are developed earlier in life, apart from the marriage, and then brought into the relationship. This is the "baggage" concept. We bring it along. Marital issues, on the other hand, are developed within the relationship. We don't start with them, and they are not brought into the marriage. Instead, we create them fresh.

The common denominator of all unresolved marital issues is resentment. Sometimes we confuse anger with resentment. They are actually two different elements (for a more thorough discussion of the differences please refer to my book *The Drifting Marriage*). Anger is a natural and healthy emotional response to hurt, fear, and frustration. Our bodies alert us to the fact that something isn't right and then energize us to deal with it. We may choose to deal with our anger and the situation in either a constructive or destructive manner. But regardless, everything is working okay up to this point. Resentment, on the other hand, is anger that fails to get resolved. Instead of dealing with a situation so as to reach closure, it goes unsettled. Our anger then begins to fester. It does not naturally go away; it remains. We begin to accumulate it.

Mistakenly, we think resentment can be held in check. Actually, it is only held in reserve. It begins to block closeness in a marriage and looks for opportunities to strike out. Scripture passages such as those below begin to make sense when we understand the difference between anger and resentment.

- If you are angry, do not let anger lead you into sin (Ephesians 4:26).
- Do not let sunset find you still nursing it (Ephesians 4:26).
- Anyone who nurses anger against his brother must be brought to judgment (Matthew 5:22).

Anger is natural and healthy. It is a normal part of who we are as God's creations. But if it doesn't get resolved, it can turn into resentment, and resentment, which is neither good nor healthy, can interfere with the growth of a marriage by blocking closeness and prompting overreaction. Was this what was happening with Marilyn? Was it resentment toward John that was fueling the intensity of her anger?

So here I was, talking with a woman whose intensity seemed to be far greater than the circumstances warranted, and wondering what was really going on. There had to be more to it than this. Was there baggage from Marilyn's personal past fueling her reaction, or was there something specifically related to her marriage? It was then that Marilyn gave me a clue.

I seem to have a "root of bitterness" toward John. It just crops up and I can't control myself. He makes me so mad!

Marilyn was referring to a passage in Hebrews where Paul cautions the brethren to be careful regarding whom they count among their members.

> Look to it that there is no one among you who forfeits the grace of God, no bitter, noxious weed growing up to poison the whole, no immoral person, no one worldly-minded like Esau.
>
> Hebrews 12:15, 16

Other translations use the phrase "no bitter root" instead of "noxious weed."

Even though Paul's focus in this passage was a little different from Marilyn's, her intent was clear. Marilyn was suggesting that she possessed a "bitter root" toward John, that she was harboring some resentment. She was beginning to look beyond the precipitating incident and deeper into herself. By so doing, Marilyn was also beginning to look at the real source of her anger, and this deeper look was revealing something from her marital history.

"Marilyn, John hurt you when he ignored your request to pray together. I understand that. But there's more to this than just that rejection. Your anger is too intense. What are you *really* mad about?"

Marilyn paused for a few moments. But then she got down to the core of the matter. Yes, she was angry about what John had done. But that was one incident. Her real anger—her resentment—stemmed from the repetitive nature of that incident. This was not the first time John had rejected her in this manner. Rather, this was his pattern—a pattern that could be followed throughout their marriage. John would never pray with her. For that matter, he would never do anything of a sensitive spiritual nature with her. Marilyn had tried dealing with this rejection in many different ways over thirty years of marriage, but usually she just said nothing. Keeping the hurt to herself, she just "stuffed" the pain and quietly developed a "root of bitterness."

Marilyn was a walking volcano. On the surface, things appeared calm, but underneath, there was immense power and energy just waiting to erupt. Finally, the release came. The proverbial straw had broken the camel's back. Marilyn's resentment could no longer be held in check, and years of pent-up feelings spewed from her like rivers of molten lava.

We're just not close spiritually! We never have been. This good, spiritual man won't pray with me. He won't have devotions with me. He won't even talk to me about spiritual matters of any kind.

I'm so frustrated with his behavior . . . with how he treats me. I've tried so many times, but he just patronizes me and goes on. He's nice, but he doesn't take me seriously.

I know John is a good man. And more, he's a good Christian man. I know he prays—at least, by himself. I know that he studies the Word. He has a wonderful testimony from the pulpit, and he's an excellent preacher. But he gives me zero!

Maybe I secretly blame him for the condition of our daughters. He never wanted to have family devotions. I don't know. All I know is I feel so alone . . . so distant from him. It's just not supposed to be this way! I know we're together on some things. But when it comes to spiritual matters—to things that really count—I don't feel close to him at all.

In all honesty, there were a number of elements operating in Marilyn's marriage that warranted attention. Interactionally, Marilyn and John seemed to have a conflict-avoidant posture. The underlying characteristic of this marital dynamic is the desire to not hurt your mate's feelings. Avoidance of this kind can have very negative consequences. In the attempt to be "nice," important issues don't get addressed. By not addressing them, there is no chance for resolution, and resentment then has an opportunity to gain a foothold in the relationship.

Another element seemed to be John's personal comfort level. He appeared to be hesitant to draw close to Marilyn emotionally. Instead, he worked hard at maintaining a safe distance which, in turn, created frustration for Marilyn.

It is easy to see how both of these factors could contribute to Marilyn's situation. But having this understanding does not take anything away from her complaint. Marilyn wanted to be spiritually close to John. She desired spiritual intimacy, and failing to have what she believed to be a legitimate part of a Christian marriage caused her great pain.

In some respects, Marilyn's case is more of an exception than it is a rule. But what makes it exceptional is only its intensity, not its occurrence. Most of the husbands and wives who speak with me about the spiritual distance in their marriages are not as angry as Marilyn was. But their number is massive. In actuality, even though Marilyn's intensity may not be the rule, her complaint probably is. I don't believe that there is much spiritual intimacy in today's Christian marriages.

I understood what Marilyn was talking about. Part of my understanding came from my experience as a marital therapist. I had had numerous discussions with many others who echoed her words:

- We can't talk about spiritual things.
- We never pray together.
- We don't share about anything spiritual.
- When it comes to spiritual matters, we're not close.

I had heard it all before. The names and the faces may have been different, but not the complaints.

Another part of my understanding came from my professional training. I was aware of the various dimensions of intimacy. I knew that drawing close to someone, in any of the intimate dimensions, requires some degree of risk. You have to be willing to be vulnerable in order to draw close. Even those who are willing to risk and invest in some areas of a relationship could find sharing something as deeply personal as religious experience uncomfortable.

So I understood exactly what Marilyn was describing—the longings, the desires, the loneliness, the frustrations, and the attempts. But my real knowledge was not coming from my professionalism, whether as a therapist or a student. My real understanding was coming from my own personal experience in my own marriage. For in an otherwise healthy, stable, growing, and bonded relationship, Jan and I had once been spiritually distant.

For fourteen years, we had had a good marriage. But it had not been a spiritually intimate marriage. All of the other dimensions of intimacy were pretty well covered: emotional, social, sexual, intellectual, and recreational. But this one had eluded us. Our situation had not been as extreme as that of Marilyn and John. It wasn't that we never dealt with spiritual issues. On occasion, we did share and pray together. But these occasions were generally precipitated by crisis or transition. Through external circumstances, we would find ourselves truly needing to deal with the spiritual aspects of our relationship. Whether it was decisions about career, the need of God's special intervention in our own life situation, or the seeking of intercession for someone else, we were circumstantially "compelled" to deal with each other. But other than on these necessary occasions, our spiritual lives remained private and separate.

The spiritual distance in our marriage was not from lack of desire on either of our parts. We both wanted the same thing: to be spiritually close (to be in tune with each other's spirituality; to be able to share what was going on in our spiritual lives; to pray together; to feel that our spiritual destinies as individuals were in sync as a couple). But desire alone did not produce what we wanted.

Interestingly, the fact that we both wanted the same thing was not readily known. We didn't realize it because we seldom talked about it; we seldom talked about it because it was too uncomfortable to deal with; and so on. It was a continuing cycle. Being uncomfortable, we seldom dealt with it. Because we seldom dealt with it, it remained uncomfortable. Being uncomfortable. . . . What we will discover later in this book is that sharing your personal spiritual journey is a definite prerequisite to attaining spiritual intimacy. It was a prerequisite that was seldom met in our marriage.

So the cycle continued and continued. Through births, deaths, and career changes; through a whole lot of living; and through both good times and bad times. Secretly, and sometimes not so secretly, we wanted things to be different, but change seemed to be beyond our power. Finally we decided to break the cycle—to take control of our lives. After fourteen years of being spiritually distant, we became *ready* to do something about it.

2
"Are We the Only Ones Who Feel This Way?"

As Jan and I began to seriously deal with the level of spiritual intimacy existing in our marriage, we made a series of discoveries. First, we found that we had not been spiritually close throughout our marriage. This was no surprise to either one of us and was more of a confirmation of fact than a discovery. Second, we found that we had both truly desired to be closer spiritually than we had been. This was a discovery because Jan had not seen me in this light. This fact led to our third discovery, that a great deal of misperception had operated in our marriage when it came to the area of spiritual intimacy.

To say *we* finally became ready to deal with the lack of spiritual closeness in our marriage suggests that neither Jan nor I was ready before that time. Nothing could be further from the truth. Jan had always been ready. It just took me a little while longer—fourteen years longer, to be exact.

From the outset, Jan had expected more from the relationship than I was willing to give. It wasn't that we didn't want the same thing. We really did. But I found sharing my true spiritual self with someone else very uncomfortable.

We shared, but as I stated earlier, it was generally only as strategic needs arose. We were unified in our desire that Jesus be Lord of our lives and direct our future. And we talked and prayed together about significant opportunities and transition points. But we were not intimate. When it came to the day-to-day sharing of our own spiritual journeys (the real test of spiritual intimacy), it wasn't there. Privacy was the rule.

Jan would want us to read something together, and I would be too busy. She would want us to pray, and I would be too tired. She would share something deeply personal, but I would not respond. I would listen intently, but my sympathetic stares were followed with deafening silence. On the rare occasions when I did respond, it was only with a summarization of what she had said, an acknowledgment, but never a personal reflection.

To Jan, my avoidant behavior communicated that I was not interested in spiritual matters and, to some extent, that I did not care about her needs. Gradually my excuses and my silence took their toll and she tired of her efforts. The requests for my involvement, the statements of her need, the times of her own personal sharing—all of these tapered off. Jan seemed to resign herself to the fact that it just was not going to happen. For whatever reason, we were not going to be spiritually intimate. Our sharing would be limited to crises.

With Jan's resignation came some resentment. This was not a seething-caldron type of problem, but on occasion it would become clear that "resignation" had not brought "resolution." Jan still desired the closeness that was missing, and the disappointment was frustrating.

So that was the situation when *we* finally decided to deal with spiritual intimacy in our relationship. I was not ignorant of the distance; I was well aware of Jan's desire. More than that, I too wanted spiritual intimacy in our marriage. But Jan had no way of knowing any of this.

Our first conversation after deciding to deal with the level of spiritual intimacy in our marriage was interesting, to say the least. What was of great interest were the inaccuracies in our perceptions. I was surprised to find the extent to which Jan felt spiritually isolated. My avoidance had conveyed the message that I was not interested in being spiritually close. This was not true, but it was what she believed. She further believed that I did not care about her spiritual needs, at least that I did not care to the extent she needed me to care. The consequence for Jan was isolation.

Jan had felt "on her own" for many years. I knew that we were not close, but apparently I thought we were closer than Jan did.

> I felt that when Mother died, the only person who really cared about me spiritually—who really prayed for me daily—was gone. I knew you cared for me. But I didn't think you were as concerned about me spiritually as I needed you to be. And I was certain you weren't regularly praying for me. I felt virtually alone.

Again, the truth of the matter was that I did care and I did regularly pray for Jan, but she had no way of knowing this.

Jan was surprised to learn that I really did desire to be spiritually close to her. There were things that had interfered with this occurring, but my heart was in the right place. She was further surprised to learn that I genuinely cared about her spiritually and that I had regularly prayed for her throughout our marriage. It was amazing that our perceptions of each other could be so accurate in some areas and yet so inaccurate in others.

It began to occur to me that what Jan and I had experienced in our own spiritual relationship was probably no different from the experiences of many others. Isn't it peculiar how we often think that we are the only ones with a particular problem? We feel no one else has experienced what we have. Thus far, my experience has taught me just the opposite. I don't think that I am too different from everyone else. If something is a problem for me, then in all likelihood, it is a problem for others as well. This being the case, I generalized what Jan and I had discovered about ourselves. By so doing, I formulated three premises that I believe fairly accurately describe most Christian marriages:

- Most Christian marriages possess very little spiritual intimacy.
- Most Christian couples desire to be spiritually close.
- Between Christian mates, there is a great deal of misperception regarding what they really want and how they really feel about spiritual intimacy.

To help substantiate my three premises, I decided to ask Christian couples about their own marriages. In order to effectively gather this information, a brief questionnaire was created. This questionnaire will be discussed in depth later in this book, because it has proven to be an excellent tool in helping couples deal with the level of spiritual intimacy in their marriages. However, for the purpose of this chapter, I want to draw from a few selected questions.

The Level of Spiritual Intimacy

My first premise was that most Christian marriages actually possess very little true spiritual intimacy. There may be a great deal of similarity in religious beliefs, and these beliefs may be of high importance. Furthermore, there may be a lot of "church talk" that takes place. But this type of interaction is largely superficial in nature. It is safe. The frequency of truly in-depth interaction—of sharing your personal spiritual journey, your fears, your victories, your defeats; of praying together; of sensing a closeness spiritually, of truly being bonded—was largely missing. To ascertain whether I was accurate in my assumption, I asked a series of questions. The first question simply focused on how mates felt.

How close do you feel to your husband/wife spiritually?
____Very close
____Somewhat close
____Neutral
____Somewhat distant
____Very distant

The average response from those couples who completed my questionnaire was "Somewhat distant." Occasionally there was a response toward the positive end of the scale, a "Very close" or "Somewhat close," but these were easily offset by responses on the "Very distant" end of the continuum. Overall, the couples tested were not reporting a high sense of spiritual closeness.

You may be asking, "Who filled out the questionnaires? Were these people from off the street? Were they even Christian?" I think these are valid questions. Let me describe the respondents. My goal was, as much as possible, to be able to compare apples to apples as opposed to apples to oranges. If my concern was what was happening within the conservative Christian community, then this was where I needed to gather my data. I needed a description of what was happening within the evangelical church, so I directed my questionnaire to that population.

All of the respondents were members of evangelical churches and professing Christians. Furthermore, age, as well as length of marriage, covered a large spectrum. They were not all young, nor were they all old. There was a broad, gentle spread. So I believe that the responses I received are fairly representative of people just like you and me.

Wanting to look at the issue of spiritual closeness a little more specifically, I included a few questions that focused not on feelings (How close do you *feel?*) but on behavior (What are you *doing?*).

How frequently do the two of you discuss religious and denominational news, i.e., what is happening at church; new church programs; what church friends are doing; "church talk"; etc.?

____Very frequently (nearly daily)

____Occasionally (weekly)

____Very infrequently (monthly)

____Almost never

How frequently do the two of you discuss with each other theological issues, i.e., beliefs about religion or doctrine, although not of a personal nature (superficial . . . not as it applies to what is happening in your own personal life)?

____Very frequently (nearly daily)

____Occasionally (weekly)

____Very infrequently (monthly)

____Almost never

How frequently do the two of you share with each other what is happening in your own spiritual lives, i.e., what God is doing for you personally (nonsuperficial sharing of personal growth, struggles, insights, etc.)?

_____Very frequently (nearly daily)
_____Occasionally (weekly)
_____Very infrequently (monthly)
_____Almost never

I listed these three questions in what I believed to be a descending order of closeness. In other words, the first question described the most superficial activity. The second question was more in depth. The last question described the least superficial behavior of the three. It was my contention that intimacy is not solely something we feel but also something we do. And referring to spiritual intimacy, with an underlying premise that we are not very close, it was my assumption that responses to these questions would reflect a gradual move from a higher frequency with the earlier and more superficial questions to a lesser frequency with the latter and more in-depth behaviors.

Not surprisingly, respondents could very frequently (nearly daily) talk about church matters, and occasionally (weekly) discuss theological and religious issues, but could only very infrequently (monthly) or almost never share with each other what was really going on in their own spiritual lives. I seemed to be correct in my assumption. When you add to these findings the responses to one last question,

How frequently do you pray together (other than at mealtimes)?
_____Very frequently (nearly daily)
_____Occasionally (weekly)
_____Very infrequently (monthly)
_____Almost never

and, to no surprise, find the average response lies between very infrequently (monthly) and almost never, it seems to suggest that my first premise about the level of spiritual intimacy in most Christian marriages being fairly low is reasonably accurate.

Quite simply, we are just not spiritually close. Marriages may appear one way from the outside looking in, but reality is far different. And rather than this being an isolated occurrence, it appears to be a very common problem. It is not just *you*—it's *us*.

The Desire for Spiritual Intimacy

My second premise was that, even though there isn't much spiritual intimacy in our marriages, most Christian couples do actually desire to be spiritually close to their mates. Again, this was based on my own experience. Jan and I had been spiritually distant, yet we had both desired things to be different. I felt we were not alone in our situation.

To substantiate my belief, I asked one simple question: "How satisfied are you?" I already knew that couples were not close. That was determined by the series of questions we have just discussed. But how satisfied were they with the distance? If they did not desire more closeness, then respondents would be satisfied with things as they were. That seemed only logical. However, if they wanted something more—if they desired a closer spiritual relationship with their mates—then there ought to be some level of dissatisfaction. So here is the question as it appears on the questionnaire:

How satisfied are you with the frequency level of personal sharing about truly spiritual matters that is taking place between you and your mate?

____Very satisfied

_____Somewhat satisfied (okay but could be better)
_____Somewhat dissatisfied (really could stand improvement)
_____Very dissatisfied

The average response was somewhat dissatisfied (really could stand improvement). Once again, my premise was validated. Jan and I had not been alone. There were others experiencing what we had experienced. Generally speaking, most couples feel spiritually distant from their mates, yet it is their overwhelming desire to be closer . . . to be intimate. They are not satisfied with the situation, yet they feel limited in how to change things. They have a desire to change but don't know how.

Misperceptions

I have already mentioned the prevalent "outside" misperception. As we look at other couples from the outside, we assume that, surely, they must not have the same problems we have. It is becoming apparent that the attitude "We're the only ones who feel this way" is inaccurate. Our experience is the norm, not the exception. But my third premise does not focus on the outside misperceptions. Rather, it addresses the misperceptions that lie within the marriage—those on the "inside." Between Christian mates, there is a great deal of misperception regarding what they really want and how they really feel about spiritual intimacy.

We have these misperceptions because we do not talk about our problems. It's as simple as that. If we honestly talked about what we want, how we feel, and what we think, there would be little room for confusion. But we don't do this. Instead, we avoid this sensitive and uncomfortable area and fill in the gaps with assumptions and guesses that soon become facts.

I addressed this issue of misperception by asking two questions. First,

What is it that prevents you from sharing personal spiritual matters with your mate?

and second,

What is it that prevents your mate from sharing personal spiritual matters with you?

With both of these questions, respondents had eight possible options from which to choose. As we will see later, the first of these two questions is very helpful in determining how to improve the level of spiritual intimacy in your marriage. Once you can identify what it is that prevents you from sharing with your mate (those things that interfere with your becoming spiritually intimate), you then have an area upon which to focus your attention. But to address the issue of misperception requires that we look at both questions and do a cross-comparison between mates.

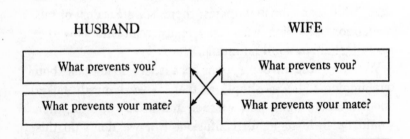

This diagram illustrates what I mean by a cross-comparison. If the perceptions between a husband and wife are accurate, there ought to be agreement between their answers. What a husband identifies as preventing him from sharing and what his wife identifies as preventing him from sharing ought to be consistent. For example, if a husband says that he isn't interested and his wife also says that he isn't interested, then their perceptions are fairly accurate. If, on the other hand, the couple is operating with misperceptions, there won't be agreement between their answers. An example of this would be a husband who says that he finds it uncomfortable to share, whereas his wife states that he just doesn't care. These are two clearly different perspectives resulting in a graphic misperception.

Upon cross-comparison, I found inconsistent responses in the majority of the questionnaires. The reasons identified by one mate for which he/she did not share personal spiritual matters were different from those assumed by his/her mate. These couples were riddled with misperceptions. So, once again, my premise was validated. There appears to be a great deal of misperception regarding what Christian mates really want and how they really feel about spiritual intimacy.

No Surprises

The findings of this questionnaire were not surprising, only confirming. I didn't think that what I had experienced in life was a great deal different from what most other people had experienced. If spiritual distance had been a problem for Jan and me, then surely it had been a problem for others as well. And this proved to be the case.

There is something reassuring about knowing that you are not alone, that you are not the first to have a particular problem or difficulty. Jan and I weren't the only ones to feel the way we did, and neither are you. In reality, it's not simply a case of either you or me having the problem. Rather, it is a difficulty that almost all of us share. And it is a difficulty that most all of us can do something about.

3
"What Is Spiritual Intimacy, Anyway?"

In this chapter, I will describe exactly what spiritual intimacy is. But in order to do this, I must move from large to small. An understanding of something as specific as spiritual intimacy must be preceded by a comprehension of intimacy in general.

Intimacy is a word that usually prompts a blush. The reason for this is that our society tends to misinterpret the word. We place more importance on its connotative meaning than on its actual definition. Whenever we hear the term, our first thoughts are of a sexual nature. Even though it is true that people who have a sexual relationship are being intimate with each other, intimacy itself is much broader than that. In fact, when looking up a definition of the word, you will find a number of meanings listed before any reference to sexuality.

Intimacy more broadly refers to "personal closeness within a relationship." The most operative word here is *closeness*. This closeness would involve feelings of love and affection. But more than feelings alone, there would be depthful knowledge of who each person really is. Gradually, an interweaving of personalities takes place, until there is a sense of bonding.

One of my core beliefs about mankind is that we are created for intimacy. We are designed to be in intimate relationship. In his book *Bonding: Relationships in the Image of God*, Donald Joy made the following statement:

> The basic thesis of this book is that *God's relationship with humans is one of intimate bonding, and that all human intimacies are "rehearsals" for the ultimate reunion of humans with their Creator.* Stated inversely, we might say that *all humans are bonding beings, such that their yearning for intimacy is an internal magnet which draws them, often unwittingly, toward God, for whose intimate relationship they are created.*

I believe Dr. Joy's understanding of our created complexity is accurate. It was the fourth-century churchman Augustine who first said that we all have a God-shaped vacuum in our hearts. Until this vacuum is filled by God, we meander through life in meaningless existence. It is only when we enter into relationship with our Creator that the void is filled. This vertical relationship, which begins with conversion, is intended to become deeper and more intimate as we journey with the Lord. Our search for intimacy with our Creator does not end with conversion; it is only in finding God that our intimacy begins.

That for which we "createdly" yearn vertically, we also "createdly" desire horizontally. In fact, our earthly (horizontal) relationships, of which marriage is preeminent, are merely tangible representations of the spiritual (vertical) relationship we experience with Christ. We are companions—sojourners—and we are created to be in intimate relationship, both vertically and horizontally.

Intimacy is really the benchmark of a marriage. It is the yardstick by which we measure the success or failure of a relationship. If a couple is developing a closer, more bonded relationship, they are moving toward the master design for marriage. If, on the other hand, their relationship is characterized by distance or stagnation, they are moving more in the direction of marital failure. An "intact" relationship guarantees neither marital health nor success. A marriage that may never officially end with a legal divorce can still be a failure. The determining factor is whether or not the couple is abiding within God's design—whether they are developing a truly intimate relationship.

Let me illustrate this by recounting one of the more unusual telephone conversations I have ever had. It was with a pastor from the northeast.

My secretary informed me that a caller was holding on one of our long-distance lines. That wasn't unusual. I frequently get calls from across the nation. She went on to say that the caller was a pastor. That wasn't unusual, either. I routinely receive calls from pastors requesting referral information, consultation, or advice regarding their own personal problems. What was so unusual about this particular conversation, however, was the caller's opening statement.

I usually answer the phone with an introduction. "This is Don. May I help you?" Ordinarily, I get a similar response. Not so in this case. Instead, in a panicked shrill came the words, "I'm scared!" There was no "Hello." There was no "My name is Doug." There wasn't even a "Good morning." The only words were, "I'm scared!" These were followed by a long silence.

I have both an earned doctorate and a number of years of experience as a professional therapist, but I must admit that this opening statement caught me a little off guard. Being ever resourceful, however, and relying heavily on my extensive training and experience, I reached deep within myself and came up with what I thought to be an adequate reply: "Why?"

To this, in a calmer but still strained voice, Doug responded, "I don't know."

Do you ever feel like starting over? Like maybe you missed out on some of the instructions? That's the way I was beginning to feel in this conversation. So I asked Doug to tell me what was going on in his life. Something had to have occurred to precipitate such a reaction. What was it? With this, he began to tell me that he had just been given some startling information. A colleague and close personal friend had resigned his pastorate, left his wife and children, and begun living with another woman.

> I've had three pastorates during the past sixteen years.
> Most of them have been in this region of the United
> States, so I've gotten to know quite a few people. This
> is the fifth time during those sixteen years of ministry
> that someone I valued as a close personal friend, as well
> as a comrade in ministry, has done this.

In the kind of profession I am in, I witness a great many affairs. I see husbands leave wives, and I see wives leave husbands. It saddens me to see the pain that is associated with marital crisis, for both adults and children. And I am sometimes even angered by blatant acts of selfishness inflicted by mates on people they have supposedly loved. But this never makes me "scared." Why had it affected Doug in this manner?

Dr. Harvey: What are you afraid of?
Doug: I'm afraid it might happen to me.

Dr. Harvey: Did you feel that way after the first time you witnessed a colleague and friend have an affair?
Doug: No.
Dr. Harvey: Did you feel that way after the second?
Doug: No.
Dr. Harvey: Then why do you feel scared now?
Doug: I don't know.

There is always a precipitant. There was a reason Doug called me: his learning of his friend's actions and his own consequential emotional reaction. There was also a reason for his fear: he had experienced the same event on four previous occasions. But at none of those times had he been struck with fear. Why now? He said he didn't know. I suspected that he did. Even if he wasn't totally sure, Doug at least had some idea. He just didn't want to talk about it. So I began to follow my instinct and asked him to tell me about his marriage. "What's it like?"

> Our marriage is stable but static—as are most of those around us. But we've been married for seventeen years. You don't expect it to be like it was when you first got married. Your marriage changes. We love each other, but we're busy. And there are a lot of pressures in the ministry.

"How much do you invest in your marriage?"

> I don't know. As I said, we're both pretty busy.

I don't like "I don't knows." They usually mean, "I don't want to say," or "Don't press me on this." People know. For some reason, they just don't want to talk about it. Doug had given me three "I don't knows." I figured he had had his limit. "Describe for me a normal day."

Well, let me tell you about yesterday. I started off at 6:00 A.M. by having coffee with one of my laymen at the diner. By the time I finished with all of my responsibilities, I stumbled into the house somewhere around midnight. Now, that's not a "normal" day, but it's not all that uncommon, either.

Doug was a successful pastor. But as he continued to describe his all-too-hectic life-style, I was reminded of another pastor who had called, and, in utter frustration, reported,

I'm "more than a conqueror" in every area of my life . . . every area, that is, except my marriage.

From Doug's description, it would be a fair assumption that there wasn't much being invested into his marriage. I think he already knew that. It was probably his recognition of the consequences of failing to invest in his marriage that had scared him so.

My guess was that, at least relationally, there wasn't much there. So I began to give him a little feedback:

Doug, you're a pastor. Let me give you a spiritual metaphor. What would your position be if a church member came to you and said:

"My relationship with the Lord is stable but static, as is the case with most of those around me. But I've been a Christian for seventeen years. You don't expect it to be like it was when you first were converted. Your relationship changes. I love the Lord, but I'm pretty busy. And there are a lot of demands on my life."

What would be your position with your church members, Doug? They all have static spiritual relationships. But, "things change. What do you expect after seventeen years?" Would you be satisfied with this position?

Or would you say, "Hold it a minute. Something isn't
right here!"

My guess is that it would be the latter. You would probably try and schedule a revival. Sure, our relationship with
the Lord changes. But it should be changing for the better. It ought to be growing deeper and more intimate, not
becoming static.

Well, *marriage is the same way.*

Doug's marriage had been failing, but its failure had not
been of an obvious nature. Doug and his wife were in the
"ideal couple" syndrome. Their marriage looked fine from
the outside. When together, they were cordial, friendly, and
active. Everything seemed pleasant enough. Not only did
things appear to be fine from the outside, but their marriage
also worked pretty well on the inside. It was functionally
satisfactory. They were cooperative. Dual careers, church re-
sponsibilities, the raising of children—all of the essential tasks
were being handled. But, even though everything appeared
good from the outside and worked fine on the inside, their
marriage was actually dying.

Their marriage was void of emotion. Both Doug and his
wife were anesthetized to feelings. There were no negatives
causing disruption, but neither were there any positives bonding them together. They were just drifting along in a lifeless,
nonintimate, and emotionally distant relationship. They were
outside the master design. Their marriage was intact, but it
was not intimate. And without intimacy—without emotional
closeness—their marriage was failing. It was this realization,
precipitated by the actions of his friend, that caused Doug to
be so frightened, as well it should.

The Many Dimensions of Intimacy

Developing an intimate relationship is the master design for
marriage. But as we just witnessed in the situation with Doug,

that is not always what occurs. Sometimes we fail to develop intimate relationships, or at least we fail to develop fully intimate relationships.

Moving from large to small, I think it is extremely important to recognize the multidimensional nature of intimacy. That is why I just used the phrase *fully intimate*. In our confusion regarding this subject, it is easy for us to view intimacy from one of two opposite extremes. We see it either too broadly—as some huge, formless, and undefinable commodity—or too narrowly, as possessing one and only one quality. In reality, intimacy is far more definable than just a sense of being close. It is also much broader than just having one quality, for example, only a sexual connotation. There are many definable elements that actually comprise an intimate relationship; many parts work together to form the whole.

Viewing intimacy from this multidimensional perspective greatly enhances our understanding of closeness in marriage. We are in a much better position to assess what is actually going on. For example, a particular couple may be close in one or two areas but distant in the others. This would mean that, even though there would be some degree of closeness in their marriage, intimacy as a whole would be fairly low. Marital intimacy is actually based on how well a couple does in all the dimensions of intimacy, not just one.

The concept of intimacy being multidimensional has been explored by numerous authors and researchers. As is the case with anything conceptual, these authors do not always agree as to what constitutes the various dimensions of intimacy. I personally focus on six dimensions. What follows is a brief description of each of these, plus some questions that may give you a feel for how you are doing in your own marriage.

Emotional intimacy When you are emotionally intimate, you "feel" close to each other. You feel emotionally supported and cared for by your mate. There is a sharing of hurts and joys and a sense that each of you is genuinely interested in the well-being of the other. Attentiveness and understanding seem to be characteristics of this dimension of intimacy.

- How close do you feel to your mate?
- Are your feelings shared with each other?
- Do you feel cared for?

Social intimacy When you are socially intimate, you have many friends in common as opposed to socializing separately. This is not to say that you do not have some separate friendships, but separate friendships are not the totality of your socializing. Having time together with mutual friends is an important part of your shared activities.

- Do you have many of the same friends in common?

Sexual intimacy True sexual intimacy involves more than the mere performance of the sex act. In truly intimate marriages, sexual expression is an essential part of the relationship. It is a communication vehicle, not just a duty. If your relationship is sexually intimate, you are satisfied with your sex life. You are comfortable with each other and do not see your activity as routine. Genuine interest, satisfaction, ability to discuss sexual issues—these are characteristics of a sexually intimate relationship.

- Are you satisfied with your sexual relationship?
- Do you consider your sex life routine?
- Can you talk together about your sexual concerns?

Intellectual intimacy Intellectual intimacy involves the sharing of ideas. In short, when you are intellectually intimate, you talk to each other. More than superficial conversations about the weather, you seek input from your mate regarding issues of importance. You value your mate's opinion and want to share your own. There is an attitude of mutual respect. Feeling put down, feeling conversations are futile, feeling as though your mate is constantly trying to change your ideas—these are absent in intellectually intimate relationships. Instead, conversations are stimulating and enriching.

- Are you able to share ideas openly?
- Can you talk to each other?
- Do you feel put down in conversations?
- Are your ideas constantly being challenged?

Recreational intimacy When you are recreationally intimate, you enjoy and share in many of the same just-for-fun activities. You have many similar interests. Whether it be outdoor activities or indoor, you like playing together. Even in the midst of hectic schedules, you find time to do fun things, and in so doing, you feel closer to each other.

- Are recreational activities done together or separately?
- Do you have fun together?

Spiritual intimacy Spiritual intimacy completes my list of the significant dimensions that join together to form marital intimacy. Determining exactly what it is, and moving from large to small, has been the focus of this entire chapter. So rather than discussing it here, spiritual intimacy will be dealt with in greater detail in the next section.

The master design for marriage is intimacy. Understanding the multidimensional nature of intimacy makes us aware that the fully intimate marriage will experience multiple intimacies. The greater the number of dimensions in which we find ourselves intimate, the greater the degree of total intimacy within our marriage.

Viewing spiritual intimacy as a part of a larger scheme is important. Spiritual intimacy may be more significant than some of the other dimensions, but it is still only a part of what constitutes a healthy marriage. It is possible for a couple to have a fairly intimate relationship and not be spiritually close. But a relationship that lacks closeness in any dimension is not fully intimate. If it is the spiritual dimension that is lacking, the marriage is missing out on a very vital and enhancing force. Truly intimate relationships include spiritual intimacy.

Spiritual Intimacy

Spiritual intimacy is not an easy term to define, but the following seems to be both practical and descriptive:

> Being able to *share* your spiritual self, find this *reciprocated*, and have a *sense* of union with your mate.

Based on this definition, spiritual intimacy is something that we *do*, something that we *feel*, and something that is *interactional*.

Sharing is something that we do; it is a behavior. It is an act of self-disclosure, of opening yourself up to someone else and privileging them with a genuine glimpse of who you really are. The variety of what can be shared is enormous. At one time it may be more of a cognitive nature: You may share your beliefs and insights. Or, delving a little deeper, you may share your misbeliefs: your doubts and apprehensions. At times you will share your feelings. This will include both the good (joy and peace) and the bad (fear and pain). There will be times of victory and growth, and there will be times of dismay, when burdens, struggles, and seeming failure weigh you down. All of this represents your spiritual self, and this is what is shared in an intimate relationship.

A *sense of union* is emotional. It is something that we feel. There is a sense of acceptance, of being known for who you really are and knowing that is okay. You know that you are cared for spiritually, that at least one person is praying for you. With this sense of union is the feeling that you are spiritually "in tune" as a couple—that this is truly a marriage.

Finally, to *find it reciprocated* implies an interactional element. You cannot stand alone and experience intimacy. That is isolation. Intimacy is not a one-person game; it requires two of you. Depthful sharing that is not reciprocated by a mate will not lead to closeness. There must be an effort by you and your mate if intimacy is to be approached. It takes two.

What it isn't   Sometimes determining what something *is* is aided by describing what it *is not*. Spiritual intimacy is being neither too close nor too far.

Spiritual intimacy is not total togetherness. This would be too close. In therapy, I refer to this as "his, hers, and theirs." He has to do his thing, she has to do her thing, and they have to do their thing. A healthy balance is necessary. As Kahlil Gibran stated in *The Prophet*, "let there be spaces in your togetherness." There needs to be a time for being alone—for being separate. There is a place for privacy in a marriage, and this must be respected.

But neither is spiritual intimacy total aloneness or separateness. In dealing with the issue of spiritual closeness in marriage, I have heard it said: "If each mate is heading in the same direction, they can't be too far apart." There is truth to this statement, but if there is no sharing of each other's personal spiritual journey, there will be no intimacy. It could be likened to railroad tracks: they are headed in the same direction, but they will never touch. In a spiritually intimate marriage, the spiritual lives of husband and wife will touch each other. And the touch is enriching.

4
"Are There Prerequisites?"

When Betty first came to my office, she was depressed and despondent. Crying throughout most of the session, she began by explaining why she was there without her husband.

> Ken doesn't know I'm here. I've asked him a number of times to go to counseling with me, but he has always refused. He says we don't need it. All I know is that I'm depressed and frustrated. I don't know what's going to happen if things don't change. I was afraid to tell him I was coming for fear he'd talk me out of it again.

A recent argument had precipitated Betty's decision to finally follow through on seeing a counselor. Ken had been working long hours that pulled him away from the home. Betty made a comment about the situation. Ken's response was, "I can't seem to please you!"

> Ken's statement just cut right through me. I was really hurt. Was I all that difficult to please?
> I got terribly depressed and introspective. I began ask-

ing the question, "Is there something wrong with me?"
It was then that I decided to talk with someone. I need
a sanity check, or reality check, or something.

Betty described a sixteen-year marriage that had been functionally sound but had probably lacked genuine closeness
since its inception. The first twelve years were spent pursuing
a common goal: the ministry. First in seminary, and then in
three separate pastorates, Betty and Ken had devoted their
energies to a noble work. But in so doing, they had success-
fully substituted the pursuit of shared external tasks for in-
ternal marital investment. They had been a team, but a team
with an external focus.

Everything was fine until Ken decided to leave the
ministry.

> I think our marriage was pretty good until four years
> ago. Since Ken stopped pastoring, we don't talk, we
> don't spend time together, and we never socialize with
> any other couples. Because of the hours that he works, I
> hardly ever see him. And we probably haven't had sex
> more than twice in the past year. What's worse is, I don't
> think he even cares.
>
> A real problem is our spiritual relationship. Religion
> had been such a part of our lives for so long. When Ken
> decided the ministry just wasn't for him, it was as if there
> was nothing further for us to talk about. Whenever I try
> to bring up anything religious, he either leaves the room
> or we get into an argument. If we could come to grips
> with this area of our marriage, maybe everything else
> would come together.

We ended the session with me scheduling an appointment
to meet with Ken. Even resistant mates will usually come
once, if for no other reason than to tell their side of things.

Ken was not pleased with having to come to my office. He made this clear from the outset of our conversation. Meeting with me was inconvenient. It required some adaptation of his busy schedule. Besides, during his twelve years in the ministry, Ken had frequently been called upon to act as a marital counselor. Based on this experience, it was his assessment that his marriage did not warrant outside intervention. There wasn't anything wrong with his marriage that a less-demanding work schedule or a little more acceptance from Betty wouldn't cure.

As we discussed Ken's perspective of the marital history, I found his statement of facts and events to be consistent with what Betty had reported. First there was seminary, followed by twelve years of pastoral ministry. It was during Ken's third pastorate that he decided he wasn't cut out for this kind of service, so he took a management position in a retail store.

> The hours are long, but I had few options. All of my training and experience was in ministry. If you're not pastoring, there's not a whole lot of vocational uses for that kind of background.
>
> Betty never has accepted my decision to leave the ministry. She found so much of her identity in the pastor's-wife role. She was raised in a parsonage and thought that was the life that we would have together. But I just came to the realization that it wasn't for me.
>
> I feel good about the decision. I'm much more comfortable in a secular job. One of these days I may find my niche as a layman. For now, I'm comfortable just attending a church. But this whole religion thing is something we can't talk about. It gets too intense.

Even though Ken described the same facts and events, he did not ascribe the same significance to them. He saw his marriage as okay, whereas Betty was in despair. I decided to challenge his perception.

> You know, Ken, there's enough distance in your marriage for me to drive a truck between you and Betty.

Ken looked a little surprised at my statement. For a few moments, he just sat back and stared. Then, after a brief pause, he stated, "I don't think things are that bad."

> You don't? Well, let's look at it and see. You don't feel close to each other at all. You don't talk about anything, you measure your sex life with an annual calendar, and you can't bring up anything of a spiritual nature. So far, you're zero for four. Do you want to try for six? [I was referring to the six dimensions of intimacy in marriage: emotional, intellectual, sexual, spiritual, social, and recreational].

Again, Ken sat silently in his chair. I figured the next move was his. Finally, he broke the silence.

> You made your point. Maybe there are some things that we need to work on in our marriage. Where do you suggest we go from here?

I suggested we meet conjointly and begin to honestly look at the marriage.

Up to this point, you have been patiently following along as I have chronicled my encounter with Betty and Ken. I first met with Betty, followed by Ken, and it was then mutually agreed that they would work on their relationship. Now, my question to you is this: Where do you think we began?

Betty had stated, "If we could come to grips with this area of our life [religious], maybe everything else would come together." Do you think I began by dealing with spiritual intimacy? Or do you think that I started somewhere else?

If you said spiritual intimacy, you were wrong. This is not where I began. It was a very important area, but we couldn't work on spiritual intimacy yet because Ken and Betty were not ready to do that.

There are certain prerequisites that have to be met before a couple is ready to work on spiritual intimacy. The most basic of these is having a stable marriage. Ken and Betty's marriage was anything but stable. As we began to delve into their relationship, we found a number of things, both individual and relational, that had blocked their marriage from growing for many years. All of these had to be addressed. Only after stability was established could progress be made toward the spiritual intimacy dimension of their marriage.

This is the norm, not the exception. We may earnestly desire a spiritually intimate relationship, but unless certain prerequisites are met, this is not likely to happen.

Five Prerequisites for Spiritual Intimacy

A *prerequisite* is "something that is required beforehand." It has to be accomplished before something else can occur. The term is most generally thought of in the context of education. For example, before you can take an advanced course in psychology, you typically have to take an introductory course in general psychology. In this illustration, general psychology would be the prerequisite to taking a more advanced psychology course.

Spiritual intimacy is far different from academic study within the educational system. But we will find that for a couple to approach this level in their marriage, they have to meet certain prerequisites. Specifically, there are five criteria that must be present before spiritual intimacy can be success-fully pursued. Unless these criteria are met, it is highly un-likely that a couple will develop this dimension of their marriage.

A stable marriage   Developing spiritual intimacy will en-hance an already stable marriage, but you cannot expect to develop something this sensitive in the midst of chaos and instability. This was the situation faced by Ken and Betty.

Your spirituality is very personal. It involves private beliefs, experiences, and feelings that are probably more private than any other area of your life. Can you imagine sharing this with someone with whom you are at odds, where, whether the conflict is open and obvious or hidden and subtle, hostility and resentment are the order of the day? How about sharing your personal spiritual self with someone you can't trust, or someone you believe doesn't care about you, or from whom you feel very distant?

You may be cordial in an unstable marriage. You may even have pleasant conversations. But these will be only of a su-perficial nature. A prerequisite to approaching what is required of a couple to be spiritually close is a healthy relationship. There must be trust, honesty, mutuality, and predictability. You must feel that your mate genuinely cares for you and your needs and is willing to "put himself out" for you if necessary. In short, you have to start with a pretty good marriage.

Similar beliefs about God and religion   No two individuals will have exactly the same beliefs, but for spiritual intimacy to exist, there must be close similarity in at least the essential elements of faith. In these essential areas where similarity exists but exactness does not, an ample degree of tolerance is called for.

It is important to differentiate between what is essential

and what is not. For example, I don't consider whether or not Christians should go to church on Sunday night to be an essential tenet of faith. As we will discuss later in this book, it can be a heated and divisive issue. But it does not *have* to be. This is not the kind of belief that has to prevent closeness. Belief as to whether Jesus is the true Son of God as opposed to one of many good religious men, or whether salvation comes by any means other than through a personal relationship with Jesus Christ, however, is a different situation. These are essential, and major disagreement about these and similar beliefs will prevent movement toward spiritual intimacy.

Your beliefs need to be significant to you Having similar beliefs does little good if they are not truly important to you. It may be that you both have long multigenerational heritages in the church and were even raised in the same denomination. Religion has long been a part of your life-style, but the role that it plays in one or both of your lives—its true significance—is minimal. If this is the case, there will be no spiritual intimacy in your marriage.

Where is your passion? Is it for drawing close to God? We invest in what is important to us, and that is what needs to be shared. Similar beliefs without similar passions will not produce spiritual intimacy.

You have to want the same thing Some things happen by accident; they are unexpected and unplanned. Spiritual intimacy is *not* one of these. If you achieve it, it will be the result of genuine intent. You will both have to want it if you are going to get it.

There is an old saying, "No man works for another man's goals."

This is especially true in the area of spiritual intimacy. Achieving it will be the result of consensus. It will have to be a conjoint goal. It's not like a vacation, where one person can be dragged along. Rather, it is a journey that requires two willing partners.

You must share your own personal spiritual journey with each other   You can be a fantastic Christian worker by satisfying those first four prerequisites. You can even be an outstanding Christian layman. But you will be no more spiritually intimate with your mate than if you were unequally yoked if you do not share your journey. This was the situation with the irate pastor's wife I referred to in chapter one. Thirty years of successful ministry did not change the fact that they were not spiritually close.

From this perspective, you can see that spiritual intimacy is not necessarily a spiritual issue. It does not have to be an indication of a lack of spirituality, just a lack of sharing. This confusion between what is the result of spirituality and what is the result of personality is part of the misperception that inundates this entire topic. To clarify the issue as we have done here is helpful. Clearly, the failure to achieve spiritual intimacy in a marriage may not be an issue of spirituality at all. Rather, the core interference frequently lies in the area of our humanity—with our personality and relational dynamics.

As we will discover later, we are all influenced, and to some extent limited by, our individuality. The topic of sharing always brings forth the issue of personal comfort levels. This issue of personal discomfort with self-disclosure obviously transcends our spirituality. But if we are to be fully intimate in our marriages, it is an area that will have to be addressed, for without the sharing of your own spiritual journey, spiritual intimacy will not be attained. It is a prerequisite.

5
"What Are the Benefits of Spiritual Intimacy?"

In one sense, referring to the benefits of spiritual intimacy sounds almost sacrilegious. It's too businesslike, as if we need to get our ledgers out and calculate the cost effectiveness of such a commodity. From that standpoint, the word *benefits* is not really a good description of what we are talking about.

It's not that being spiritually intimate doesn't have any benefits. It definitely does, both personally and relationally. For example, I benefit personally in two ways. First, being spiritually intimate helps "keep me on task." It aids me in my quest to seek first the Kingdom. Staying close to Jan spiritually helps me maintain a focus on spiritual priorities. There is a reminding factor, an accountability. In this instance, we keep each other straight. Second, spiritual intimacy helps me know who I am spiritually. There is something beneficial in verbalizing what I think and feel. It is clarifying. I need Jan as a sounding board.

Spiritual intimacy also pays dividends relationally. I mentioned earlier that marital intimacy is multidimensional, that there are many parts making up the whole. The condition of any part influences the others and thus the entirety of marital intimacy. So if there is a high level of intimacy in the spiritual dimension, it cannot help but aid the overall stability of the marriage.

As we can see, spiritual intimacy definitely has its benefits. But as functionally aiding as these may be, the real benefit is in the *quality* that this dimension brings to the marriage. The true essence of love occurs with the development of a spiritually intimate relationship. This definitely changes the depth of our love. Omit it, discard it, or avoid it, and you will truly miss the potential for unfathomable blessing. In short, spiritual intimacy is "having God's best," and God's best is not something that you want to miss.

Part Two
Getting Started

6
The First Step: Assessing Your Level of Spiritual Intimacy

The first step in constructively dealing with this area of your marriage is for you to thoroughly assess your current level of spiritual intimacy. This is accomplished by both of you completing the Spiritual Intimacy in Marriage Questionnaire. Later in this chapter you will be given specific instructions as to just how to do this. For now, however, I want to explain exactly what this assessment will accomplish.

It will determine whether the necessary prerequisites have been met You cannot begin your journey toward spiritual intimacy unless you are ready. Part of being ready is having met the essential prerequisites. The Spiritual Intimacy in Marriage Questionnaire will verify that this has been accomplished.

Earlier, I listed the five prerequisites for spiritual intimacy. Actually, you could be at this point in the process with only four of those being met. If you have a stable marriage, similar religious beliefs that play a significant role in your life, and you desire to be spiritually intimate, you have met the essential prerequisites to proceed. If you have also been sharing your personal journey on a consistent basis, you have already been developing intimacy in this area. The sharing criterion seems to be the bottleneck in many otherwise ready relationships. It will be this last prerequisite dealing with sharing that will receive much of the emphasis of this book.

It will determine whether there is any confusion in your perception of each other Do you really know what your mate wants or does not want? Do you really know what stops him/her from sharing? Do you really know how your mate feels about his/her own personal spirituality, much less that of your relationship? This questionnaire will clarify all of these questions.

You may find that you know each other very well. On the other hand, there may be some surprises and discoveries. Either way, whether through confirmation or enlightenment, you will be moved further in the direction of dealing with your spiritual intimacy.

It will identify the specific elements interfering in your relationship Sharing our spiritual selves, or rather the lack of our sharing, is the bottleneck for most of us. We hold this in common. But what specifically prevents you and what specifically prevents me may be greatly different. Not everyone will have the same problem. This questionnaire will identify the specific element that acts as an interference in *your* relationship. This will allow you to give it direct attention.

It is hard to treat something that remains nebulous and undefined. "I know we ought to share more, but we just don't do it. I don't know why. We just don't."

As we clarify the problem, we can focus on solutions. For example, you treat personal discomfort different from the way you do concerns about spiritual preparedness. The key is clear identification of the particular interference. Then you know what to address.

It will challenge any denial that may be existing in your relationship   What we say is true and what is actually true are not always the same. When incongruity exists between what is stated and what is real, we frequently call this "denial." Sometimes this incongruity is known. That is when we intentionally try to fool others. At other times, however, the incongruity is unknown. It is at times like this that our minds use denial to fool ourselves. This enables us to avoid something that we don't want to face.

The way that we deal with denial is by confronting what is said or believed with reality—with tangible facts. For example, I recently saw a woman who was separated from her husband. I will refer to him as John. They were considering reconciliation. She reported a problematic marital history highlighted by a long list of irresponsible acts on his part. However, he was reportedly interested in "making some changes."

When I met with John, a different attitude emerged. His opening statement to me was, "I feel pretty good about who I am." Throughout our conversation, he kept reiterating his belief that he was an emotionally healthy and normal individual. It seemed as though John was trying to convince both me and himself of that. I allowed him to relate his history, which was sordid, and then had him complete a psychological test. Then, armed with the information that he had volunteered and the test results, I began to state facts.

> John, you are twenty-five years old and contemplating your third divorce. You have been involved with "other women" during all of your marriages, including this one,

and have a history of running from anything that may cause you pain. You stay emotionally distant from people and have periodic drinking binges. In addition, the psychological test you took suggests there are a number of areas that warrant legitimate concern.

Now, you may choose to continue to believe that you are normal and healthy. But that's not how it appears to me. The facts state that you aren't. You can face it, deal with it, and possibly change it. Or you can continue to fool yourself. But if that's your choice, you can only expect your future to be as tumultuous as your past and present.

Confrontation with facts does not always break through well-entrenched delusional systems, but in this case, it did. John agreed that there were some things in his life that continued to interfere with his being able to establish a healthy relationship. I referred him to a Christian psychologist who began working with him on his personal problems.

Sometimes we operate in denial regarding this area of spiritual intimacy in our own marriages. At times, it is known; at other times, it is not. Regardless, honestly completing this questionnaire allows us to look at the facts. We can choose to fool ourselves when we answer the questions and allow denial to continue. But if we want to work toward having God's best in our lives, we will answer the questions truthfully and then look at the facts.

It will begin the process of your dealing directly with each other A key element to developing spiritual intimacy in a marriage is for a husband and wife to deal directly with each other. Although all of the assigned tasks in this book will require your conjoint involvement, this is the first.

You could have read this book separately up to this point, but now you will have to begin dealing with each other. As you work through the first task, sharing your respective responses to the questions making up the questionnaire, the process of actually dealing with each other will commence. You will begin to talk and share about the level of spiritual intimacy in your marriage, and this will be constructive.

Task

Your first assigned task has three parts. I want you to complete the entire task now, before continuing your reading. The remainder of this chapter will describe how others have responded to the questionnaire. Since you will have already completed the questionnaire, you will be able to compare your findings. But again, do this *after* you have completed the task, not before.

Complete the Spiritual Intimacy in Marriage Questionnaire   Located in the back of this book are two copies of the Spiritual Intimacy in Marriage Questionnaire. One of these is the husband's form and the other is the wife's form. Remove the copies of the questionnaire from the book for use at this time.

The first part of the task involves your completing the questionnaire. This needs to be done *independently*. Don't work together, compare notes, or discuss either the questions or your responses as you work through the questionnaire. Be honest, be thoughtful, and take as much time as you need.

Share your questionnaire results with each other   You will do the second part of your task together. Beginning with the first question and proceeding through the last, share your respective answers. It is okay to talk about the responses at this time (your surprise, agreement, confusion, and so forth); however, don't get bogged down here. The goal of this second part of your task is clarity. You want to see how you each view things.

Discuss your findings Part two was more of a reporting of information. It was enlightening. Part three will focus on couple interaction and themes. Together, you will begin to talk about what you have learned about each other and what you would really like to see happen.

The following questions can act as a guide for your discussion. You are by no means limited to these; they are only a catalyst. Feel free to add your own. After completing this final portion of your task, proceed with the chapter. See how you compare with others who have completed this questionnaire.

- Do you believe the prerequisites for spiritual intimacy have been met? Why or why not? If not, which are lacking? What can you do about it?
- Is your reporting of the facts different or similar? Is there consistency in how you view the basics of your marriage, such as length of time as Christians, degree of marital satisfaction, frequency of sharing and praying, and so forth?
- How accurate were your perceptions of each other? Was there consistency regarding what prevents you and your mate from sharing (questions 15 and 16)? Was this surprising or confirming?
- Was there only one interference, or were there multiple ones? How many things stand in your way? Were there any that the questionnaire omitted?
- What is the consensus of opinion regarding your level of spiritual intimacy? Did your opinion change between the time you began the questionnaire and the time you completed it?

How Others Have Responded

My intent at this time is to only summarize the trends obtained from answers to questions 1–14 but to discuss in more detail the responses to questions 15 and 16. There are three reasons for this obvious display of favoritism. The first is simply readability. It is far easier to summarize the less-essential data in a brief narrative statement.

My second reason for only briefly discussing these questions is that some of the information found in the first fourteen questions has already been discussed in chapter two. Finally, it is questions 15 and 16 that really warrant our attention at this juncture. Much of the focus of the first fourteen questions was dealt with in Part One of this book. What remains to be addressed and what will be dealt with in Part Three of this book are the interferences. The interferences to spiritual intimacy are the focus of questions 15 and 16.

Questions 1–14

Respondents represented a broad age range and were evenly distributed as far as length of marriage. The average couple reported that they:

- were fairly satisfied with their marriage
- had at least similar religious beliefs
- had religious beliefs that were important to them
- were both Christian (length of time varied)
- at best, were somewhat distant regarding how close they felt to each other spiritually

The average respondent couple could very frequently engage in church talk and could occasionally discuss theological issues but could only very infrequently or almost never share personal spiritual information or pray together. There was an increasing degree of personal discomfort as the topics became less superficial. It was far easier to talk about church than it was to talk about what God was doing in their lives personally.

Finally, most respondents were at least somewhat dissatisfied (really could stand improvement) with the frequency and level of personal sharing about truly spiritual matters taking place in their marriage.

Questions 15 and 16: The Interferences

The final two questions dealt with interferences. "What is it that prevents you/your mate from sharing personal spiritual matters?" I will focus mainly on the first of these questions: "What prevents you?" Reference will be made to the second question, "What prevents your mate," only as it applies to the issue of misperceptions.

Question 15   All percentages in the diagram below are based on the first choice only. Some respondents listed more than one interference, others did not. It was less confusing to focus only on each respondent's most significant interference. I have also separated the responses according to sex, which suggests some interesting trends. Answers will be listed according to their overall endorsement by respondents, not as they actually appeared on the questionnaire.

If you were not able to answer "very satisfied" in question 14, what is it that prevents you from sharing personal spiritual matters with your mate?

	Percent	
	Male	Female
____I find it too uncomfortable to share something that personal.	35	19
____I'm not spiritual enough to share.	28	15
____Is there a reason I have not listed? ["time"]	16	21

	Percent	
	Male	*Female*
_____I get tired of sharing when my husband/ wife will not share with me.	3	30
_____I think my husband/wife does not accept my spirituality and does not allow me to be who I am. He/she is critical.	9	3
_____I feel good about my personal spiritual relationship but do not see the need to share with my husband/wife.	6	6
_____My husband/wife is not interested in listening to what I have to share.	3	6
_____My husband/wife is not spiritual enough for me to share with.	0	0

Interference #1: I find it too uncomfortable to share something that personal. Personal discomfort with sharing something as sensitive as spiritual matters was identified as the greatest single overall interference. Although this was identified as a problem by both men and women, husbands identified it twice as often as their wives. One-third of the men stated that this is why they do not share.

Interference #2: I'm not spiritual enough to share. Similar to the last response, this was identified by both men and women. But again, husbands identified it as an interference about twice as often as wives did. It is interesting to note that even though this concern about a personal lack of spirituality was the second overall complaint, all of the respondents said they were Christians.

Interference #3: Is there a reason I have not listed? ["time"] Not everyone thought the questionnaire omitted an option. But when they did, they all agreed on the same thing: time. "We don't have the time." "We don't take the time." "We don't schedule the time." There were many variations of the same theme. Respondents seemed to feel that their hectic life-

styles interfered with their sharing. Time was stated enough
to rank third overall and was fairly evenly distributed between
husbands and wives.

*Interference #4: I get tired of sharing when my husband/wife will
not share with me.* Although only fourth on the overall list, this
was because of the lopsided difference in the sexes. Women
rated this as their most frequent reason for not sharing,
whereas men scarcely mentioned it at all. Nearly one-third of
the wives listed this as their number-one interference.

*Interference #5: I think my husband/wife does not accept my
spirituality and does not allow me to be who I am. He/she is critical.*
Although receiving less response than the front-runners, it is
interesting to note the difference by sexes. Men listed this as
a complaint more frequently than did women, just as they
responded to another spirituality question: "I'm not spiritual
enough to share."

*Interference #6: I feel good about my personal spiritual relation-
ship but do not see the need to share with my husband/wife.* This was
another less-identified reason for not sharing. Interestingly,
there was no sex difference. Husbands and wives checked it
evenly.

*Interference #7: My husband/wife is not interested in listening to
what I have to share.* This received a fairly low rating. It would
appear that, even if husbands won't "respond" to their wives
(wives' primary complaint), they at least will "listen" to them.

*Interference #8: My husband/wife is not spiritual enough for me
to share with.* This item received no checks, an interesting
finding when you consider that so many mates felt they were
not spiritual enough to share.

Question 16 The benefit from examining the reasons mates
thought their spouses did not share was not in determining
the single greatest perceived interference; rather, it was in

seeing how accurate their perceptions actually were. Was the reason a wife thought her husband did not share actually the reason given by her husband, or was it something altogether different? As it turned out, there was a greater likelihood of misperception than of accuracy.

Two predominant misperception patterns emerged. The first involved a view commonly held by wives of their husbands. Fifty-two percent of the male respondents said that their primary reason for not sharing was either their personal discomfort or their lack of spirituality. Is this what their wives said about them? Generally, no. Rather, these women frequently perceived their husbands as spiritually sound but not having the need to share. Obviously, there is a great deal of difference between these two viewpoints.

The second misperception pattern revolved around this purported reason for a mate's failure to share: "He/she does not believe I am spiritual enough to share with." This was a frequent response, yet at no time was that indicated as a reason for not sharing by either a husband or a wife. It was perceived to be a problem, but it was not—another clear case of misperception.

Moving On

Well, how did you do? Did you discover anything that you didn't already know about each other by completing the first task? Were there any surprises, or just confirmations? How did you compare with typical respondents? Were there similarities or differences?

I hope this exercise has not only been enlightening but has also allowed you to focus on a common concern: your spiritual intimacy. If so, you are ready to move on to the next step. Have fun!

7
Turning the Corner: Choosing to Be Close

If you are going to have spiritual intimacy in your marriage, you have to "go to Jerusalem."

Luke is my favorite Gospel writer. I like his tendency to be precise—his attention to detail. We seem to see more of this in Luke's Gospel than we do in those of his cohorts.

This difference in writing style is noted in the recording of Jesus' pivotal turn toward Jerusalem. There is a sense that Jesus' entire ministry was a journey to Jerusalem. He occasionally spoke of it as "destination" and "destiny." But this was in terms of "one of these days" and "in the future." The time was not yet "right." He was not yet "ready." In those earlier years, Jesus was content to travel through the Galilean and Judean countrysides, ministering to people and investing in the lives of the disciples.

Then things changed. The preparation time had ended. It was time to move toward His destiny—the reason that He came to be the God-Man. It was time to go to Jerusalem.

This was a monumental time in Jesus' ministry and greatly significant for the future of mankind. And how was this pivotal historical event recorded by the Gospel writers? Matthew records the turn toward Jerusalem like this:

> Jesus was journeying towards Jerusalem.
>
> Matthew 20:17

Mark states it about as simply:

> They were on the road, going up to Jerusalem, Jesus leading the way.
>
> Mark 10:32

Both authors go on to say that Jesus took the disciples aside and explained the events that would take place in Jerusalem— the arrest, the condemnation, the death, and the resurrection. But there is no attention given to the significance of the decision to now change the focus of Jesus' ministry. It is as if they were all on a guided tour and the next stop happened to be Jerusalem. At least, there is no attention given other than by Luke.

To Luke, there was more than just events taking place, and he wanted to make sure that we understood the significance of what had occurred. Luke captured the essence of the turn toward Jerusalem when he stated:

> As the time approached when he was to be taken up to heaven, he set his face resolutely towards Jerusalem.
>
> Luke 9:51

Why did Jesus "resolutely" turn toward Jerusalem? Why did He not just "journey" toward Jerusalem as recorded by Matthew, or simply be "on the road" as indicated by Mark? Why a resolute turn? The answer is simple: Jesus turned resolutely because He knew what lay ahead. He knew the betrayal. He knew the mocking. He knew the disappointment, the abandonment, the aloneness. And He knew the pain. He knew what was to come, but it was time, so He resolutely set His face toward Jerusalem.

Jesus was concerned that His disciples understand the need for being resolute. He was so concerned that He gave three examples, all recorded by Luke, illustrating precisely what being resolute is and precisely what it is not:

> As they were going along the road a man said to him, "I will follow you wherever you go." Jesus answered, "Foxes have their holes, the birds their roosts; but the Son of Man has nowhere to lay his head."
>
> To another he said, "Follow me," but the man replied, "Let me go and bury my father first." Jesus said, "Leave the dead to bury their dead; you must go and announce the kingdom of God."
>
> Yet another said, "I will follow you, sir; but let me first say good-bye to my people at home." To him Jesus said, "No one who sets his hand to the plough and then keeps looking back is fit for the kingdom of God."
>
> Luke 9:57–62

The first illustration is of a man they met along the road who said, "I will follow you wherever you go." What was Jesus' response to this statement of allegiance? "Foxes have their holes, the birds their roosts; but the Son of Man has nowhere to lay his head." At first, I found Jesus' response puzzling. What has it got to do with anything? But when I realized that Jesus' focus was on being "resolute," on what goes into our making decisions, it became clear. Jesus' decision to turn toward Jerusalem was not made flippantly. He knew what was going to take place. He understood the costs. And with this knowledge, He chose to move toward His destiny. It was with full awareness and not out of ignorance. He wanted the "man on the road" to do the same:

> Don't give me an easy, hasty, automatic response. These are the facts. Be sure. Evaluate; count the costs; look at the situation; calculate. And with full fore-thought, then make your decision. Don't make it flip-pantly, because much will be required of you. Are you sure that you are ready?

Resolute decisions are not based on ignorance. They are based on reality. And Jesus wanted the man on the road to realistically assess the situation. If, after counting the costs, and in spite of the difficulties, his decision was still to "follow you wherever you go," then his decision would have been resolute.

This example is followed by two "yes, but first" illustra-tions. Two men are separately asked to follow Jesus. Both are willing, but there is other pressing business that first requires attention. Jesus' responses in both of these situations are acts of clarification as to exactly what being resolute is not. To the first He said, "Leave the dead to bury the dead." And to the other He said, "No one who sets his hand to the plough and then keeps looking back is fit for the kingdom of God."

If you are going to follow Jesus, it requires a resolute de-cision, not a flippant one or one based on ignorance but a well-informed and well-thought-out commitment. And not one with divided loyalties, as respectable as these other re-sponsibilities may be. *Resolute* means being ready to follow, regardless.

What does all of this have to do with spiritual intimacy? If you are going to become spiritually intimate in your mar-riage, you have to "go to Jerusalem." In other words, you have to *choose* to be close—not flippantly, not halfheartedly, but resolutely.

If being a therapist has taught me anything, it is this: "Things change not because they become easy but because we become resolute."

Whether it be personal problems or dissatisfactions within our relationship, if we are content to wait until things get easy, the likelihood of any significant change is doubtful. Things change because we honestly face ourselves and assume responsibility for what we find. We become ready to take control of our lives.

Changing Your Relationship

You have assessed your situation, so you are now more aware. You know what interferes with your relationship, and you understand what needs to be changed. But are you ready to proceed? Are you ready to make the necessary changes required if you are to grow closer spiritually?

Any change that occurs in your relationship will take place as a process that is preceded by a resolve. I grappled with the correct word to use here. *Crisis* sounds too traumatic, and words such as *decision* and *choice* are too mild. What I am attempting to describe is an occurrence similar to religious conversion. In conversion, there is a pivotal point where good intentions and genuine desires are recognized as not being good enough, where at last a genuine commitment is made to Jesus Christ. Some call this a decision for Christ, others refer to it as a crisis experience; they mean the same thing.

Religious conversion is more than a mere rational decision. It is also emotional. Yet this emotional aspect is not always surrounded by overwhelming, traumatic reactions. It can be quiet and peaceful. To me, *resolve* is a word that finds descriptive license here. It encompasses a blending of the intellectual and the emotional. When people resolve to do something, they have thought it through, and they feel deeply about their decision. They are committed, and that's what takes place in conversion. What was has passed away; all things are new. Conversion brings a change in direction and the beginning of a changed life.

The readiness to become spiritually intimate is similar to that of a conversion experience. You have to have thought it through, and you have to want it—*both* of you. If only one of you is ready, it probably will not take place. Remember, Jan was ready to become spiritually intimate when we first married. It was fourteen years before I, too, was ready. When we both became resolute, our journey toward spiritual intimacy began.

With the genuine resolve to become spiritually intimate regardless of whatever difficulties you may encounter comes the opportunity for change. This change will not be instantaneous. Instead, it will be of a gradual nature. That is what is meant by *process*. It takes time to grow. But that's normal.

Most of the remainder of this book will focus specifically on ways to help you change your relationship. Some of this will involve constructive ideas for designing your own regimen for sharing. Other chapters will offer suggestions for dealing with some of the interferences that hinder your growth. But this will be of little benefit unless you are both ready to proceed.

How is your resolve? Are you ready to proceed? Do you really want to be spiritually intimate? Are you resolute about your decision? Is there consensus? The task at the end of this chapter will help you answer these questions. But be advised, all of these questions need to be answered affirmatively if there is going to be any change in your relationship. Resolutely, you have to choose to be close. You have to be ready to "go to Jerusalem."

Misconceptions Interfering With Growth

Before proceeding to the task, I want to briefly discuss three common misconceptions that can impede the growth process. Some of these will be dealt with in greater detail later in this book. However, this chapter is a turning point. It is important that you proceed with as little encumbrance as possible.

"It's all going to be easy now"   True, there must be resolve before there can be process, and with resolve comes the opportunity for growth. But process is slow, and growth of any kind can be demanding.

Change is seldom instantaneous. But with resolve comes potential. You are now ready to gradually take control of what has appeared to be beyond your grasp. Give growth effort and time.

"My mate and I will grow at the same rate"   You are two different people. Just because you both want the same thing does not mean that you will grow at the same rate.

Do not be overly concerned if your individual spiritual growth or your ease in sharing grows at different paces. Just be responsible for yourself and continue to share.

"We have to see things totally the same way"   Once again, you are two different people. Even though it is important that you have similar religious beliefs, there are no two people who will always view things in exactly the same way. Granted, there are times when beliefs are so different that they are considered deviant. Obviously, deviant beliefs are not acceptable, but this extreme is not usually what troubles us.

Friction often arises over beliefs that are slightly different from your own. Beliefs that are different from yours should not be considered wrong just because they are not the same. Allow for individual diversity. Be accepting. The most important issue is the personal relationship you and your mate each have with the Lord. Do not let picky theology get in the way.

Task

There are two parts to this task. The first part involves decision making, whereas the second will give you an opportunity for sharing.

Please bear this in mind: Anything disclosed in this task is totally confidential. It is to be kept solely between the two of you. Furthermore, you should begin and end with affirmation. Begin with a statement acknowledging your love for each other and a willingness to accept whatever is said during the discussion without defensiveness. End with a physical affirmation such as a hug or kiss.

Discuss your readiness to proceed Spend fifteen to twenty minutes (more if needed) discussing your feelings about being spiritually intimate. Even though it may seem frightening, is this something that you both want and need? Is the "want to" there? Are you resolutely willing to deal with those things that might interfere with your attaining this level of marital closeness? If so, make that commitment to each other.

Share your spiritual journey Take some time to share your testimony. Begin with how you became a Christian and proceed to the present. You may want to use a time-line concept as a model. Pause to discuss significant events that have influenced your spiritual development, events that you may see differently now than when they occurred.

You may be thinking that your mate already knows this about you. Possibly he or she does, but I doubt it. At least, your mate probably does not know it from your present, more mature outlook. Do you really know that much about each other spiritually? Here's your chance to find out. Enjoy your exploration.

8
Developing Your Plan: Structuring Your Intimacy

Some individuals don't like the idea of structure, especially as it relates to an area as personal as intimacy. They ask, "How can you *make* something like intimacy occur?" They want to be freer. "Isn't intimacy something that you just naturally feel? Isn't it spontaneous?"

When I use the term *structure*, I am not suggesting that we are going to artificially create anything. Rather, we are working together to provide an environment for growth.

Intimate *experiences* can occur spontaneously. These are unexpected, out-of-the-blue times when something happens to cause us to feel close to each other. Maybe a service at church is unusually blessing, or possibly God intervenes in our lives in a special way. An overwhelming heart of praise then prompts a time for sharing. These kinds of experiences occur in each of our lives. We are thankful when they occur. They are definite boons and blessings, but they are incidents, not patterns. They are brief glimpses, as it were, of a far better existence, but they are not the sum and substance of an intimate relationship.

Intimate *relationships*, as opposed to intimate experiences, are the result of planning. They are built. The sense of union that comes with genuine spiritual closeness will not just happen. If it is present, it is because of definite intent and follow-through on your part. You choose to invest, and do. It's not left to mere chance.

An ironic thing occurred when Jan and I began to develop a more spiritually intimate relationship. The frequency of purely spontaneous experiences increased. Rather than infringing upon closeness, structure enhanced it. Through structure, our relationship grew. With growth, there was freedom, and with freedom came a greater opportunity for spontaneity.

Whereas some do not like the idea of structure, others like it too much. Have you ever noticed how some people always seem to know exactly what you "ought" to do? When I was in high school, I was a long-distance runner. It was not unusual for me to run more than one hundred miles a week in training. A knee injury ended my competitive capabilities, and running was given up for other pursuits. Twenty years, three degrees, a wife, two children, and a career later, I decided to pick up the sport again. When I did, everybody had suggestions on how I needed to train. At least, they had suggestions for me if I wanted to "do it right."

One friend told me that I needed to run in the early morning: That's when "real" runners run. There's just something about morning that makes it best. Another informed me that I needed to run every day: to miss even one day of running was to lose my edge on conditioning. A physician friend and fellow runner suggested I alternate my training: run one day and ride a bike the next. This was best because it allowed me to cross-train. Another advised that I focus on distance and not necessarily speed: the further you run the better. That builds endurance. It is far more important than how fast you run.

Needless to say, I had more suggestions for the correct way to train than I knew what to do with. So whose advice did I follow? Basically, I ended up doing what worked best for me. In view of my age, physical limitations, schedule constraints, and goal for running, I developed a plan that I could both live with and enjoy. Consequently, I run every other day (even at the loss of conditioning); I run at a brisk yet comfortable pace, preferring this over the methodical jog for longer distances (even at the loss of endurance); and I run in the heat of the day (even if "real" runners train in the morning). This may contradict what many think are better ways, but it works best for me.

When you start looking at spiritual intimacy, you will probably also find a host of friends with well-meaning advice. Just as with my running, they will know exactly what you need to do. You will need to have daily Bible study together, or you will need to pray together every day, or. . . .

The point I am making is this: Even though moving toward spiritual intimacy will require some structure (a plan of action), the parameters around how this will actually play itself out in your marriage are broad. There is no absolute right or wrong when it comes to developing a plan. What is right is what works for you. What works for you may not work for me, but it doesn't have to. It only has to work for you.

Having established that there is no absolutely right or wrong way to develop a plan, let me offer a model that Jan and I found helpful. It is offered only as a suggestion. You may try it and then offer your own adaptations. That's okay. What is more important than what you do is that you do it. Plan and do something that works for you.

A Suggested Model for Your Plan of Action

As you begin to develop your plan of action, use two benchmarks as a guide. First, as we just discussed, your plan should meet your needs and not the needs of others. Second, develop a structure that is accomplishable. Do not be overenergetic or too idealistic. It will be far better for you to start small and then choose to enlarge than to be forced to cut back. Allow yourself to grow into something else if the need arises. Let the process work.

The model Jan and I used had only three parts. The first of these was the most extensive. You will find these listed below with some explanatory comments.

Meet to discuss weekly   In order to give our life some structure, we found it imperative to set a time to meet together. To meet on a daily basis would have been a monumental undertaking, yet to focus on our joint spiritual life less than weekly seemed too disconnected, so we settled on a weekly time together.

This time together was then etched in stone. There are many legitimate activities that vie for our attention. The same is true in your situation. We had to predetermine that our time together would have priority. It was placed on our respective calendars, thereby guaranteeing it was a legitimate part of our week. It became a very special time that we began to look forward to.

Things to consider when determining your time together are your opportunities for privacy and your own energy level. If you are a night person but your mate drifts off after 9:00 P.M., then 10:00 P.M. probably won't work too well for you. If you have young children who don't go to bed until 8:00 P.M., then 7:00 P.M. probably won't work, either. There may be no time that is ideal, but be realistic. Some times will be better than others. Together, come up with a place that is comfortable and a time that offers you privacy and finds you having enough energy reserve to relate. Then commit to it.

During this time together, there will be a number of things you will want to do.

Ask the question, "Are we ready to start?" Jesus' advice from His Sermon on the Mount is applicable here:

> If, when you are bringing your gift to the altar, you suddenly remember that your brother has a grievance against you, leave your gift where it is before the altar. First go and make your peace with your brother, and only then come back and offer your gift.
>
> Matthew 5:23, 24

Is there anything standing in the way of your sharing together? Something that has not been dealt with during the week? Something in need of confession and forgiveness? If so, make peace so you can move on.

Begin with prayer. This is a prayer of invitation, and it can be brief. You are inviting Jesus to be a part of what you are doing and asking for help as you focus on truly spiritual matters.

Share what is going on in your life spiritually. This should be viewed as an opportunity, not a demand. Take this opportunity to talk about your spiritual self: your goals, your struggles, and your growth. Share what the Lord is telling you, or share that He's been silent. What are you learning? Where is your confusion? What are your frustrations? These are the things you need to be talking about.

There will be intense times—times of overflowing. There will also be dry times, when you feel not much is taking place in your meeting together. There will be uneven times when you will be up and your mate will be down or your mate will be up and you will be down. All of this is okay. It is the normal ebb and flow of life. Do not think you will always be on an emotional high.

When meeting together, be sure to share how you are *feeling* and not just what you are thinking. Genuine self-disclosure requires that you do both. Talking about your feelings may be a new experience, but it will be rewarding. It helps you understand each other, to really get to know your mate. There is nothing more rewarding.

Deal with some content that you have in common. Being directly introspective can be a little heavy or wearisome, especially if this is the focus week after week. A sense of lightness can be brought to your meeting together if you will deal with something concrete. This can be accomplished by having some subject or topic, whether formally or informally, upon which to focus your attention. For example, you may identify forgiveness and the way it has impacted your life as an area of discussion. During the week, each of you will then get into the topic independently and bring your thoughts together during your designated time for sharing. This would be an informal means of dealing with content.

More formal means would be to deal with tangible aids. For example, during your time together, you may choose to:

- Study the Bible together. Here you would select an area of Scripture to read and share together.
- Study a Bible aid together. Here you would select and read a commentary or other explanatory book regarding Scripture.
- Read an inspirational book together. This would not necessarily be biblical in nature. But there are many Christian works dedicated to spiritual growth and inspiration.

- Read a Christian subject matter book together. Here you would choose something with a topical focus such as forgiveness, sin, spiritual gifts.

Something important to bear in mind, whether you are utilizing content formally or informally, is that the content itself is not the primary goal. You are using content as an opportunity to share yourself. It is a vehicle for discussion. Always reflect on how this content applies to you. What is the Lord saying to you in the Scripture? How can you identify with what the author of a book has said? How does it affect you? It is only in becoming personal that content takes on meaning and significance.

End with prayer. Your prayer at the beginning was brief and inviting. Feel free to spend more time now in gaining suitable closure to your time together. I don't want to presume to tell you how to pray, but some of the areas to be included could be:

- Pray about what transpired during your sharing.
- Pray about your commitment to draw closer spiritually.
- Ask the Lord to help you to deal with those things that interfere with your developing a more spiritually intimate marriage.

Things to remember during your time of sharing

Balance the talking. Few couples are evenly balanced when it comes to talking. One tends to talk more, or better. Consciously make an effort to even things out.

Be affirming and accepting. As much as possible, this should be a positive experience. Let this be a time when you can be open and vulnerable without fearing that your mate will condemn you for how you feel or think. Behave as Christ would behave.

What this time together is not:

- This is not a time to discuss the running of the household.
- This is not a time to discuss children.
- This is not a time for catching up with what has been going on, other than how this pertains to you spiritually.
- This is not a time to discuss grievances you have with each other.
- This is not a time to talk church.
- This is not a time to talk theology. You can talk about theology all day long and say nothing about your own personal experience.
- This is not a marital-counseling session.

All of these areas I have just listed are legitimate topics for discussion, but this is not the right time. The focus now is on sharing your spiritual life, and anything that diverts you from this goal, no matter how worthy it may appear, is to be resisted.

Expect to be assaulted by Satan. Developing a spiritually intimate marriage is a tremendous goal. It can bring high spiritual rewards. Anything with this potential will obviously prompt resistance from the enemy of our souls.

If you select Monday evenings to meet because it has historically been a free night, you can expect something beyond your control to change this, and it will probably be something legitimate, such as church board meetings or the creation of a visitation program. That's the way Satan works. Don't be alarmed—just prepared to face the resistance through prioritization and, where necessary adaptation. Remember, greater is He that is in you than he that is in the world.

Commit to pray for each other You need to know that you are prayed for. Even though I had always prayed for Jan and she for me, neither of us really knew the extent to which this was done. When we decided to deal with the spiritual intimacy in our marriage, the clear knowledge that we were being

prayed for on a daily basis became a part of our commitment.
Regarding our spiritual relationship, I pray for the following
on a daily basis:

- Jan's specific needs: difficult situations, her spiritual
  growth, her emotional and physical well-being, and
  any needs she brings to my attention
- myself as a mate and to be the spiritual partner she
  needs
- my marriage
- our respective sensitivity to each other's personal
  needs

Jan knows that she is prayed for, and so do I, and this enriches
our marriage.

Commit to pray together   Many of the considerations that
played a role in the selection of your sharing time together
also figure into this decision. Your frequency needs to be
accomplishable, and your time and place need to be both
convenient and private.

Jan and I chose to start small and enlarge as opportunity
presented itself. We meet on a weekly basis. There are spontaneous times during some weeks when special needs prompt
additional times of prayer together, but the weekly meeting is
fairly consistent.

We deal with issues surrounding our spiritual life together,
such as our own idiosyncratic interferences, emotions, clarity
of focus, honesty without vindictiveness, and so forth. But
this shared prayer time is not limited to our spiritual relationship alone. We also deal with practical concerns, petitions, the
needs of others, and our own praises and thanksgiving. This
time together has added to our spiritual joy.

Final Thoughts

Dorothee Soelle made the following observation in her book *Death by Bread Alone*:

> Theories about religious experience, such as Laing's journey or Jung's descent into depth-consciousness, are merely tools, aids by which to test one's own experience. *Each step of one's own is worth more than all the knowledge and insight of others* [italics mine].

Although she is referring to one's own individual spiritual journey, the same can be said of your journey toward spiritual intimacy.

I can make suggestions, I can discuss benefits, I can even share what has happened in my own marriage and what I believe can happen in yours. But of far more value is for you to begin to take your own steps. Spiritual intimacy will not come from what you read, but from what you do. And your own experience will be the most meaningful to you.

Task

You are committed to drawing closer together spiritually in your marriage. Now, how are you going to do it? Here is your opportunity to develop your own personal plan.

Below are some suggested parameters to help you develop a workable plan of action. Use these as a discussion guide as you work together. Things to remember are:

- There is no right or wrong.
- You need to design a plan that is workable (accomplishable).
- This is a conjoint effort. Therefore, you need to be in agreement on the final product.

Have fun working and growing together.

Meet to discuss weekly   What is your commitment to meeting weekly? Some suggestions are:

- Schedule a time.
- Decide whether or not you are ready.
- Begin and end with prayer.
- Share what is going on in your life spiritually.
- Deal with some content (books, Bible, and so forth).

Commit to pray for each other   What is your commitment to pray for each other?

- What is your frequency?
- How will your needs be made known to each other?
- What will be the focus of the prayer?

Commit to pray together   What is your commitment here?

- What is your frequency?
- When and where will this occur?
- What will be the focus of this prayer time together?
- When will exceptions be warranted?

9
What if Your Mate Isn't Ready?

Knowing what couples ought to do is the easy part of working with marriages. Husbands and wives ought to be investing in their marriages. They ought to be giving; to be unselfish; to be self-disclosing; to set healthy boundaries and have legitimate expectations of the relationship. They ought to deal honestly and directly with each other regarding feelings, whether positive or negative; to be willing to put themselves out for each other; to be forgiving. In short, they ought to be developing a bonded and intimate relationship.

Over the years, I have observed that a broad gulf often exists between what ought to be going on and what actually occurs. When it comes to making changes in a relationship, making adaptations from "what is" to "what ought to be," I find that couples will do only what they are ready to do.

In therapy situations, couples seldom come to counseling actually prepared to work on their relationship. They may think they are ready. They often even tell me of their willing intent. But seldom is this the case. Generally, they are stuck in their respective positions, resistant to change. So it is my initial responsibility to get them unstuck, or to get them ready. Sometimes I am successful in this effort. At other times, however, I am not. In the latter situations, little immediate headway can be made in the relationship.

I remember counseling a couple who came to me at the request of their pastor. Their relationship could better be described as an endurance test than a marriage. In fact, what struck me most in that first session was their countenances. Twenty-five years of fighting had taken its toll. As true "weary warriors," they were both tired and worn out.

Tom and Sue came to counseling because of a specific problem they were unable to resolve. Tom wanted to do one thing, and Sue was opposed. As we discussed the history of their relationship, it became clear that this present issue was actually a metaphor for their marriage. This was the way everything was handled: Tom would decide, and Sue would oppose.

Sometimes this type of power struggle is the result of partners who each want to control their mate. But as we spent more time together, it became clear that wasn't the case with Tom and Sue. Instead, we had one mate, Tom, intent on being in control. And we had another, Sue, equally intent on not being controlled. It wasn't that Tom had to do things Sue's way, but Sue was determined that she wasn't going to always do things his way. She wanted to count, to have some say in things. But for Tom, it was either his way or no way.

I began to deal with Tom regarding his need to control Sue and the impact this behavior had on his marriage, but he rejected my assessment of what was taking place. From his perspective, everything would be fine if Sue would just stop resisting him. There was no need for him to change any of his behavior, much less his attitude.

After five sessions, Tom decided that counseling was not doing their marriage any good, so they stopped coming. Occasionally, I would get a phone call from Sue as things between them continued to deteriorate, but after a few months, even that contact stopped.

I surmised that they probably got a divorce. That's what Tom had threatened to do during each of the counseling sessions. Imagine my surprise when I saw them together about two years later at a marriage seminar I was conducting. Not only were they together but they also appeared happy. What was going on? During one of the breaks in the program, Sue approached me.

> I bet you're surprised to see us here together. Well, things got pretty bad there for a while. Tom moved out and took all of the money. He was trying to force me to do what he wanted. I probably would have divorced him, but I couldn't even hire an attorney.
>
> Then it happened. He changed. Out of the blue, Tom came home, said he had been wrong, and wanted to start over. And he meant it. That's all it took for me. It's been great ever since.

I was elated to hear the news, but I was also curious as to what had prompted the change in Tom. So I asked the pastor who had originally referred them to me if he knew the story.

> I thought they were going to get a divorce. I spoke with both of them while they were separated, but it seemed hopeless. Then a man Tom had known for a few years took him aside and began to talk to him about his role as a husband, and specifically, how he had failed. He told Tom that he had been controlling and selfish throughout the marriage and that he was about to lose his

wife and family and had no one to blame but himself. What he said had an impact. Tom went home to Sue, and things have been different ever since.

I don't understand all there is to know about readiness. Why is it that when I told Tom he was controlling and selfish, he resisted my statements and stopped coming to counseling? But when someone else told him the same thing only six months later, he embraced these words as truth and changed his behavior. Was it how he was confronted? Was it the timing? Did this other man have more influence than I? Did the events during the six months have something to do with it? Was it a combination of all the above, "one sowing, one watering, and one reaping the harvest"? I don't know. All I do know is that people can only do what they are ready to do and, for whatever reason, when Tom finally got ready to change, he did.

Perhaps you are facing a situation where only you are ready to proceed toward a more spiritually intimate marriage. You would like to share and pray together—to sense the specialness that comes from being spiritually close. But for some reason, your mate isn't ready to make that commitment. What do you do? Without a combined effort, there will not be much headway made toward spiritual closeness. But is this any reason to give up? Is there anything you can do?

The answer to this is yes. Even though you cannot force your mate to become more spiritually intimate, there are things you can do to aid his or her readiness. Likewise, there are other things that need to be avoided. You are not responsible for making things happen, but you can aid in the readiness of your mate.

Aids to Readiness

An important part of marriage is determining what you are and are not responsible for. You are not entirely responsible for making the marriage work, but you are responsible for your part. You are not responsible for how your mate behaves, but you are responsible for how you behave.

This differentiation of responsibility underscores the theme of this section. Your goal is to responsibly act in a manner that allows your mate the best opportunity to get ready for a more spiritually intimate relationship. Whether this will actually occur is difficult to say. People do not always get ready at the same pace. But we still need to be responsible for our part.

Aid 1: State your needs and desires directly There is nothing wrong with stating "I need" in a marriage. In fact, it is considered a sign of a healthy relationship. We all have needs and desires. Even though some of these may not always be legitimate, the fact remains that marriage is based on expectations, yet frequently these needs go unstated.

I refer to the failure to state needs and desires directly as "weak signaling." There are a number of inaccurate attitudes that inadvertently support this problem. The first is, "My mate ought to know." This is a classic excuse for weak signaling. The reasoning is that if my mate really loved me or cared enough or was truly sensitive to my needs, he or she would know what I need. In actuality, this attitude is akin to expecting mind reading. I think you would agree that this expectation is somewhat unreasonable.

A second inaccurate attitude is, "It's inappropriate to ask." With women, this attitude emerges as false femininity. "Why, it would be highly unladylike to express needs." They believe that true ladies are pleasant, demure, and sweet, and to ask for attention is totally unacceptable. With men, the attitude emerges as extreme machismo. Not only do real men not eat quiche, neither do they express needs. You never heard

Rhett Butler or "The Duke" talking about their needs. Neither will these husbands.

A third inaccurate attitude is, "I'm just too easygoing." This is a kind way of describing what is in reality a totally nonproductive behavior. Being too nice or being passive are more accurate descriptions. Passive mates deny their own personal rights. They deny their right to have needs. By so doing, they also deny their right to have them met.

In a healthy relationship, there must be statements of need. These statements should be clear and direct, yet not attacking. "I statements" seem to work the best. For example: "I need to feel close to you spiritually." Or, "I feel spiritually distant from you. Is there anything we could do about that?"

On the other hand, statements such as, "You are always so closed," or, "Why can't you share with me?" can be easily perceived as personal attacks. There are times when these comments can be very appropriate. But the present goal is to give opportunity for readiness, and this is best accomplished with statements of need, not attacks.

Your goal is to make your mate aware of both your need for closeness and your availability to move toward this goal when he or she is ready. Therefore, what he ought to sense from you is this: "I am ready when you are."

Aid 2: Do not pursue   Pursuing a mate merely pushes him or her further away. Remember, your goal is to provide an opportunity for readiness. Constantly pushing and shoving usually works against this end.

There are two pursuing tactics that need to be avoided. The first is blatant harassment. Jan is a social worker by profession and has repeatedly assured me that harassment works wonderfully in her field. That may be the case in social services, but it has poorer results in marriage. Constantly pointing out your mate's failure and your disappointment will probably not encourage him to move toward you emotionally. Harassing a mate pushes him away; it does not draw him closer.

The second pursuing tactic is less obvious than harassment. It involves saying all the right things, but they are said too often. For example, stating your desire and need for spiritual intimacy is a very appropriate thing to do. However, if you state it daily, it becomes harassing. The repetitive nature is what makes it inappropriate, not the words themselves.

Allow your mate some space in which to grow. An occasional reminder is sufficient. He has a better memory than you think. Your goal is not to force anything upon him; you are merely aiding his movement toward readiness.

Aid 3: Model what you want What is it that you want from your mate? Basically, you want him or her to invest in you spiritually. Do you remember our definition of spiritual intimacy?

> Being able to *share* your spiritual self, find this *reciprocated*, and have a *sense* of union with your mate.

If genuine mutual investment is taking place, the sense of union will be there also. One is the natural consequence of the other. The key rests with both mates sharing their spiritual selves. The problem is the lack of readiness on the part of one mate.

To suggest that you model what you want is to say that, regardless of what your mate is ready to do, you need to continue in "well doing." You need to *demonstrate* the very thing you would like in return. In short, you need to continue sharing your spiritual journey. Be willing to talk about how God is leading in your life; what God is saying to you; what you are learning. Share your spiritual frustrations, fears, and praises.

This type of behavior on your part invites your mate to respond. It is not pursuing, demanding, or harassing. Rather it is helping to establish a comfortable context whereby he or she can feel free to enter in. It is inviting.

The reason I stress this point is the feedback I received from my questionnaire. The statement, "I get tired of sharing when my husband or wife will not share with me," ranked fourth overall as an interference for spiritual sharing within marriage. But, as noted previously, this fourth-place ranking was due largely to lopsided difference in the sexes. It was actually the greatest single reason for wives' not sharing. Nearly one-third of the wives responding to the questionnaire listed this as their number-one interference. Therefore, it can really become a problem.

If you want to aid your mate's readiness to become spiritually intimate, as opposed to interfering with it, you will continue in "well doing." You will demonstrate what you actually want in return, not so much as a learning device but as an invitation. You want him to feel free to enter in.

Aid 4: Invest in the other areas of your marriage   Spiritual intimacy is an important aspect of a relationship, but it is not the only aspect. We do not need to lose sight of the fact that there are many other areas of a marriage, all interacting at the same time.

At times it can be easy to lose our perspective and fail to recognize these other dimensions of marital intimacy. To neglect the emotional, intellectual, sexual, social, or recreational areas of your marriage just because the spiritual is not what you want it to be is unwise. Remember, one of the prerequisites to spiritual intimacy is marital stability, and this is measured by how well you are doing in all of the areas of your relationship, not just one. Spiritual intimacy will enhance an already stable relationship, but it is not likely to occur in a greatly unstable one.

You may have a mate who is not yet ready to pursue closeness in the spiritual realm, but that does not mean you cannot have a stable and enriching marriage. Feeling good about the relationship in general could be an encouragement to draw close in this other, more special, way.

Invest in your marriage—all aspects of it. This will aid your mate's readiness for spiritual closeness.

Aid 5: Do not become resentful Resentment creates barriers between people. That is the opposite of what we want to see happen in marriage. What we really want is for mates to draw closer together.

Resentment is the by-product of unresolved anger. A common scenario in couples I see would be that of a wife becoming frustrated with her husband. She wants a closer spiritual relationship, but he tends to keep his spirituality to himself. This disappoints her, but she says little about it. Instead, she "stuffs" her feelings, thinks he doesn't care, and begins to become resentful.

Stating your needs, as we discussed before, will help alleviate some of this frustration. It is constructive, whereas stuffing is totally nonproductive. But there is a second factor that also needs to be considered. Much of our initial frustration comes not from what we are getting or not getting but from the meaning we attach to it. For instance, just because a husband is not sharing his spiritual journey with his wife does not mean that he does not care about how she feels. Nor does it mean that he does not desire the same kind of relationship as she does. All that behavior tells us for sure is that he either is or is not doing something.

Looking back at the results of my questionnaire, the greatest misperception between mates applies directly to this subject. Wives frequently perceived their husbands as having neither the need to share nor an interest in sharing with them. Yet their mates never stated this. Instead, they indicated their hesitancy to be the result of either a personal discomfort with sharing or a feeling that they were not spiritual enough to share. Obviously there is a great deal of difference between what these wives perceived and what their husbands reported.

To view your mate as insensitive and uncaring can be greatly disillusioning. But to view him as caring but limited by his own personal difficulties is far less frustrating. I think the data supports this second perspective more than it does the first.

Resentment is an interference, not an aid, to readiness. It is far less frustrating and far less resentment building to view your mate as caring but limited rather than capable but insensitive. Remember your goal: You want to aid his readiness, not prevent it.

Part Three
Dealing With
the
Interferences

10
"I Find It Uncomfortable to Share"

There are many interferences of spiritual intimacy from which to choose, so why have I elected to begin this section with personal discomfort? This particular interference received the greatest overall response in the questionnaire. The specific statement was:

> I find it too uncomfortable to share something that personal [personal spiritual matters].

With 35 percent of the husbands and 19 percent of the wives identifying personal discomfort about sharing as their number-one interference, it would appear that our "ease" at closeness is something with which many of us may have to reckon. But my selection of this particular interference was based on more than questionnaire results.

The questionnaire results that gave personal discomfort the highest overall rating were not surprising. In fact, they were expected. Yet, as high a rating as this area may have received, I believe this problem is actually larger than these results suggest. For, to one degree or another, personal discomfort with sharing is something with which we all grapple.

Those who checked off this questionnaire statement may have been indicating that personal discomfort was their primary interference. But even those who identified some other reason as a more significant interference could probably have listed personal discomfort as a second or third choice. Personal discomfort speaks to the issue of individuality, and our own individuality is a problem that must be faced by us all.

We Are Alike yet Different

One of the problems with any book of this nature is that it tends to generalize. By this I mean that it tends to view each of us as being the same: thinking the same, feeling the same, having the same set of problems, and so forth. I focus on what we share in common as if we were all alike, instead of looking at us as separate individuals. In reality, we are not the same but are, in fact, all uniquely different. No two of us are exactly alike.

So how do we reconcile two propositions as diverse as these, one stating that we are all the same and the other that we are all uniquely different? I think reconciling these two positions comes with recognizing that one fits inside of the other.

We are first and foremost similar. This is the larger picture. And it is this fact that allows me to write a book like this. We all have the same basic needs for security, to love and be loved, to experience intimacy within relationships, to have a sense of knowing who we are, to know God, and so forth. Within these outer boundaries of commonality, our individuality is displayed. How we resolve the issue of security, how we love and are loved, the degree to which we experience intimacy, how we see ourselves, whether or not we find God

—these issues of individuality form our personal uniqueness.

Placing individuality within the context of our commonality is likened to the tuning of a violin. It is the pegs at the end of the neck of the violin that bring the strings close to pitch. They set the basic limits. But the fine-tuning is accomplished by turning the small metal tuners located near the bridge. These screwlike tuners correct or allow minor deviations.

Even our uniqueness is within normal limits. We are far more similar than we are dissimilar. The fact that this book is written generically only means that you may have to do some adapting. There will be parts that fit you well. There will be others that do not really apply to your situation. But these will usually be matters of degree. You will need to fit the book to your particular circumstances.

Even though our uniqueness is generally within normal limits, I think it is important that we understand the significance of what we bring to a relationship. Although typically within normal limits, we are still God's "peculiar" people. As much as I would like to simplistically focus only on our similarities, we cannot ignore that within our peculiarity lie differences. We are not alike. I will focus on commonality throughout most of this book, but be aware that you bring uniqueness to a marriage, and sometimes uniqueness has its limitations.

I do not intend to deal thoroughly with this area of individuality. That would constitute a book in itself. But even if we give it only minimal attention, we need to recognize that who we are as individuals has a lot to do with what we develop within a relationship. When mates say to me,

> I know I should talk with Jane about "personal stuff."
> But I've always had difficulty with self-disclosure. It's far
> more comfortable just to keep things to myself.

or,

> Our relationship probably would be better if I talked
> to Bill about my dissatisfactions. But I've never wanted
> to hurt anyone's feelings, much less my husband's. I
> guess I would prefer to avoid conflict if at all possible.

they are referring to their uniqueness, not to something that is
standard behavior for everyone. Yet their uniqueness, even
though it may be fairly normal behavior, can interfere with
their attaining God's best for their marriage.

Being normal does not mean we are perfect. We may wish
to be perfect. We may even try to be perfect. But if life has
taught me anything, it is that we are normally imperfect.
There are characteristics that are positive about us, but there
are also those that are negative. We are a composition of both.
Being imperfect means we have some limitations—and some
of us are more limited than others.

As normal adults, one of the ways we vary is in our capacity
and desire for intimacy. Quite simply, some of us need more
space than others. Stated inversely, some of us are more uncomfortable with closeness than others. Granted, there is
some flexibility allowed. You can have a different need for
closeness than someone else and still be healthy. But frequently these variations act as personal limitations. They limit
our ease at achieving the intimacy for which we are designed.

Capacity for Closeness

We are all influenced, and to some extent limited, by our
individuality. This limitation is probably most evident in this
area of our own personal capacity for intimacy. We seem to
emerge into adulthood, after a plus or minus passage through
childhood and adolescence, with a fairly well-established

"comfort level" for interpersonal closeness. Drawing close to someone can be uncomfortable. As a client once remarked, "Intimacy is a scary thing." Another said, "Sometimes the thing I want the most is the thing I can stand the least." They were both reflecting on comfort levels.

Tolerance for Closeness

This diagram graphically depicts what I mean by variable comfort levels. Most of us fall somewhere in the center portion of the diagram. We have a normal capacity for closeness, which also means that we will have some normal difficulties as well. There will be areas of discomfort as we develop intimacy within our marriages. A few individuals will fall somewhere far to the left side of the diagram, meaning that their comfort level with sharing is high. They will find it easier to establish an intimate relationship. Others will fall far to the right of the scale, demonstrating very low tolerance for closeness. For them, intimacy will be a much more difficult task and, in extreme cases, probably unlikely.

Reasons for Discomfort

In therapy situations, we frequently talk about the *whys* and the *whats*. The whats are the behaviors: what is happening. The whys are the motivations: why you do what you do. Whats can be singularly identifiable (you can observe one particular behavior), but whys can be multiple. It seems as though an endless number of rationales can be conjured up explaining why a particular behavior occurred.

Some people do not see the need for determining the whys. They suggest you only focus on changing the whats. Others say that if you focus solely on the whys, the whats will take care of themselves. My personal position is somewhere in the middle. I believe that having an understanding of why we do what we do is important, but we can't stop there. Once we understand, we need to act. We need to take responsibility for what we find.

There are many factors that work together to influence our personality development, but when it comes to looking specifically at our capacity for closeness, none seem to be more significant than our self-concept and the things we learn at home.

Your self-concept Self-concept refers to just how comfortable you feel about yourself. If you feel fairly secure about who you are, closeness is an easier task. If, on the other hand, you feel insecure, intimacy becomes more difficult. It's really quite understandable. To draw close to another person requires self-disclosure, sharing who you are with them. This involves more than just superficial conversation about football or the weather. It is in-depth personal "stuff" about you. How do you feel about things? What is your opinion? What do you really believe? What is important to you? What do you fear? Do you express your true and honest self? These are the characteristics of "personal stuff" as opposed to superficial.

People are like onions, not apples. When my daughter was young, she liked to eat apples, but she disliked the peelings. So Paige would always ask me to peel the apple for her before she ate it. That was a simple enough task. After only a few seconds of work, the entire meat of the apple was ready for consumption. An onion, however, can be peeled all day. Its consistency is entirely different from that of an apple. Rather than having only one exterior layer, an onion is layered to the core. It is nothing but one layer on top of another. That's the

way people are. We, too, have many layers. If we deal with
only "insignificant stuff," we stay on the top layer, never
delving deeper into who we really are. Our relationships are
characterized by superficiality. It is only as we delve deeper
that movement toward intimacy begins.

So what does any of this have to do with self-concept?
Simply this: In order to share, you have to be willing to take
a risk. When you take a risk, you are being vulnerable—
opening yourself to possible pain through rejection, being
ignored, ridiculed, abused, and so forth. In order to be vulnerable, you have to feel pretty good about who you are. The
inverse order is this: "I feel good about myself, so I am willing
to become vulnerable by taking a risk and honestly sharing
something personal about myself."

Gradually, layer by layer, you share yourself with your
mate. As you find your sharing reciprocated, your movement
toward bonding begins. But it is a journey that is either made
easier or more difficult by the way you view yourself.

What you learn at home   We learn a lot of things at home,
in our families of origin. Some of what we learn is intentionally taught. Examples of this would be manners, how to make
our beds, to show respect to others, and to attend church. We
also learn through observation. This is less intentional than
the more directive examples listed above. Observational learning is usually thought of as modeled behavior. It ranges from
simple tasks to complex roles. For example, you can learn
how to wash a car by watching your father do it. Or, again by
watching your father, you may begin to define exactly what a
father does, what his role is, by observing how he plays the
part throughout the years of your youth.

Direct instruction and modeling are two important ways in
which we learn at home, but they don't necessarily speak to

the issue of emotional comfort levels. With emotional comfort levels, our learning is far more experiential. Rather than being directly taught or observing the behavior of another person, we develop emotional comfort levels by learning to live within the context of our family.

To "live" states it too simply. More accurately, we learn to survive. We survive home, and we do so through accommodation. Just as we learn to live in all kinds of weather conditions, so we adapt to the prevailing emotional attitudes in the family. If home is a place where parents are nurturing, feelings are respected, and there is safe opportunity for open and honest sharing, we learn to be comfortable with emotions. If, on the other hand, home is less than this, emotions become an unwelcome liability.

We are survivors: we do what it takes to maintain some level of personal safety and comfort. Just as we all have the need for closeness, we are all born with a need to be emotionally safe. We are self-protective. It is at home, in our families of origin, that we learn to balance these two needs. Sometimes we learn all too well that closeness is threatening and distance is safety. We are out of balance. But this is what we have learned, and it is with what we have learned that we are most comfortable.

When we leave home, this learning is not left behind. To the contrary, we carry it with us into our adult relationships. We learn well. Without concerted efforts to change, what we learned to do at home will be naturally and comfortably replicated throughout adulthood.

When I first met with Tom and Pam, probably the best term to describe them was tired. They were literally worn out. For thirty years, their marriage had been characterized by tension. Pam had anxiously pursued Tom, trying to get the closeness that she longingly desired. Tom, on the other hand, had skillfully dodged her attempts at closeness, maintaining for himself a comfortable emotional distance. The harder Pam pressed, the further Tom moved away. He would withdraw both emotionally and physically. There were days when he would scarcely say a word. As Pam pulled back and became preoccupied with her own life, Tom would reestablish contact. Cordiality would resume, and the functional aspects of the marriage would continue. When Pam would tire of the superficiality and make a move toward Tom for greater intimacy, he again would pull away. It was as if they were performing a dance, with each of them following prescribed steps. But thirty years of dancing had taken its toll.

> I'm so tired of this. I feel like leaving Tom and just forgetting the whole thing. I love him, but I just can't live with him like this.

And what was Tom's response?

> I've never been able to satisfy Pam. I can't do anything right. I don't believe I could ever do enough to make her happy. She wants too much. I feel like I'm getting "the third degree" when she gets in one of her moods.

Who was right? Did Pam want too much? Was she too needy? Or did Tom want to give too little? Was he too emotionally closed, too self-protective?

There's not a pat answer to this question. It really depends on the situation. Sometimes it can be a little of both. For example, a needy woman may marry a closed man. Or it may be that one mate may have some reasonable and healthy expectations for either closeness or space but the other finds himself or herself further down the continuum. Either way, the same pattern emerges.

When you know what constitutes a healthy, growing relationship, you can begin to assess a marriage by comparing what ought to be happening with what is actually occurring and expected. That is what I did with Tom and Pam. What did Tom want out of the marriage? What did Pam want? What was actually happening? Who was doing what?

As I began to get answers to these questions and observed what Tom thought was demanding behavior and what Pam described as closed and aloof, the accuracy of perception seemed to be favoring Pam. What she wanted from Tom appeared to be quite legitimate. Granted, her reaction to Tom was occasionally excessive. In fact, at times it bordered on harassment. Tom's avoidance could be exasperating. But ordinarily Pam was cool, calm, and collected. All she wanted was for Tom to invest a little of himself in the marriage, to deal with her on an emotional level, and to allow some sense of closeness to develop.

Tom, however, felt uncomfortable with emotions. He wanted Pam to be part of his life. In fact, he felt quite alone whenever they were apart. But he did not want to have to deal with anything involving feelings. If Pam could just be around the house, or talk only about superficial matters, then Tom was content. At those times, he felt close enough to be secure in the relationship but still distant enough to maintain personal safety. He was comfortable.

> I like living with Pam when she's not pressing me. At home, we can watch TV together. Or I can work in my wood shop while she putters around with whatever it is that she likes to do. Pam goes to ball games with me, and that's always fun. And the few weekends that I've gone to the lake cabin fishing without Pam were real lonely. I like her to go wherever I go. She just needs to lighten up a little and not press me.

We generally acquire our personal comfort levels honestly. I was sure that Tom would prove to be no exception. Somewhere he had learned to be closed and distant. I assumed it was at home, so I began to ask him questions about his family background.

Tom described his home as good. I found that good meant stable. Tom was an only child, and his physical needs were well provided for by his parents, but there was no warmth in the home. Both parents were professionals with careers and interests of their own. Their marriage was functionally sound but lacked emotional involvement. His parents were always cordial and cooperative toward each other, but during the eighteen years preceding his departure for college, Tom never witnessed any signs of affection. What they apparently felt uncomfortable displaying toward each other, they likewise withheld from Tom. There was cordiality and material concern, but there was no nurturing—no times of sharing hurts, no one to listen to disappointments, no one with whom to talk deeply about the fears of growing up.

As Tom grew older, he and his father developed a better relationship. They shared activities in common. But as they fished or played ball together, Tom was careful to keep the conversation light. Sensitive areas were avoided, and they never talked about feelings. "I always knew Dad loved me. He just had a hard time showing it." This was the good and stable home in which Tom had learned to survive.

Tom was provided for, but he was not *cared* for. At least, he was not cared for the way he really needed. Some children grow up in homes where abuse and neglect are everyday occurrences. They don't know what safety is. Others are fortunate enough to never experience these negatives. All of their functional needs are more than provided for. But the truly privileged children are those who have safety, security, and nurturing. This last quality, whether or not there is true emotional investment, is what differentiates being genuinely cared for from being merely provided for. Tom had been well provided for, but he had not been cared for.

Tom had learned well. And what he learned at home he replicated in his marriage. It was natural, it was automatic, and it was comfortable. Without thought, Tom's need for safety and emotional comfort overruled his need for closeness. He was comfortable with the distance; it was what he had learned at home. Tom was not willing to risk his personal comfort for the possibility of an enriched relationship.

It is not just in homes like Tom's that we learn to value self-protection over the benefits of closeness. Sometimes this is learned in homes that are more chaotic in nature. When you share how you feel and it gets you in trouble, or it gets you rejected, or you are laughed at and ridiculed, or you are taken advantage of, or any number of other possible negative reactions, you learn that it's not safe to share. You find that trusting can be dangerous, so you learn to withhold. This keeps you safe and comfortable.

Whatever the particular characteristics of your home, and whatever it was that you learned there, you carry it with you. Just because you leave home and move into a safer relationship does not mean you are going to forget what you have learned. We learn to survive home, and we don't forget it. We can deal with it, we can change it, but we don't forget it.

Making Choices

To some extent, we are all limited in what we have to offer to our marriages. Who we are definitely influences what we can attain relationally. None of us possess self-concepts that have been unscathed by the experiences of life, and none of us come from ideal families. We are all survivors. But our personal limitations speak to the issue of ease, not inability. Although we have our idiosyncratic differences, most of us have what it takes to achieve intimacy. We fall within the normal limits, and for those of us who dare, even the limitations that we carry with us can be adapted.

Our capacity for closeness can change. Maturity, positive experiences, an improved self-concept, insight into nonproductive patterns, a better understanding of emotional health—all these can decrease the influence of our limitations. But for most of us, it will ultimately come to the issue of choice.

Your feelings of discomfort may be quite legitimate, but this legitimacy does not warrant nonproductive behavior. The goal of awareness and understanding is not to blame others or to find excuses for ourselves. Rather, insight allows us the opportunity to take charge. How long will you continue to allow comfort/discomfort to control your life? When will you take control?

Health is facing self and taking responsibility for what you find. It is doing what is needed in the best interest of your relationship as opposed to what is natural and comfortable. If we are to pursue intimacy in our marriages, there will be times when we will be confronted with our personal discomfort. What will we choose? Will it be safety and security? to withdraw? to be closed? Or will it be to risk, to share, and to draw close? If our goal is intimacy, the choice is clear: We will do what is in the best interest of our relationship, instead of doing what may seem to be the most comfortable. We will invest in our marriage.

Task

Not one of us is perfect. We all have some chinks in our armor. For some of us, the chinks may be represented by feelings of discomfort when it comes to sharing personal information or feelings about ourselves. Feeling uncomfortable is no disgrace. Frequently the whys for our hesitancy are well-founded and somewhat legitimate. However, what is unfortunate is allowing this personal discomfort to control our lives and block our achieving all that God has in store for us in marriage.

The first part of your task is written. In order to deal constructively with this interference, I would like you to construct some sort of rationale for why you feel the way you do. This will require some thought, effort, and a willingness to get inside yourself. You may want to draw from some of the influences discussed in the chapter as contributors to your particular situation. On the other hand, maybe you have some thoughts of your own. At any rate, develop a rationale of understanding and write this rationale down on paper.

After developing your rationale, write out how this interferes with your present attempts to be spiritually intimate in your marriage. The final part of the written portion of this task is for you to state what you intend to do in order to take control of this interference. What is your commitment?

The second part of this task allows you the opportunity of talking to each other. After writing the three-part narrative, I want the two of you to share your respective narratives by conducting a back-to-back exercise. To do this, you will need to go to a private room in your home and place two comfortable chairs back-to-back. Take a seat and let the more verbal of you begin by reading his or her narrative, followed by any additional comments he may wish to make.

Each of you will have ten uninterrupted minutes. You may decide how to use your ten-minute segment. If you wish to use only part of the time, then the remainder of your ten minutes is to be spent in silence. When the first ten-minute segment is completed, the other mate may begin the next ten-minute period. After you have both had your turn of un-interrupted time, you may turn your chairs toward each other and have a normal discussion.

Have fun in your self-discovery!

11
"I'm Not Spiritual Enough"

When we combine the two statements from the questionnaire, "I'm not spiritual enough to share" and "I think my mate does not accept my spirituality and does not allow me to be who I am. He/she is critical," we find approximately one-third of the reported interference in sharing for men, and one-fifth of that for women, to be represented by these issues. And this response was from a totally Christian population.

Would you have thought that feelings of nonspirituality would be a primary reason for Christian mates to refrain from sharing within their marriages, or, even if they did feel good about their own spirituality, to be hesitant due to a sense that their personal confidence was not shared by their mates? I can understand how these two attitudes could definitely limit the sharing between husbands and wives, but what I question is the legitimacy of their presence.

I intend to deal with each of these attitudes separately. Spiritual unworthiness will be addressed in this chapter and the issue of nonacceptance by a mate will be addressed in the next. But the theme I will follow is the same for both: Not only are these attitudes nonproductive, they are also illegitimate.

What follows are three considerations that directly confront the legitimacy of the attitude, "I'm not spiritual enough to share." After all is said, I think you will agree with me that feeling spiritually unworthy, although sometimes a very real feeling, is at best an illegitimate attitude.

Considerations

Wherever you are in your own spiritual journey (growth process), you have something to offer   For Christians, the statement, "I'm not spiritual enough to share" is never accurate. Wherever you are spiritually and whatever is going on in your life are important. It's important because it's *real* and it's where you happen to be.

What some may mean by "I'm not spiritual enough" is that they believe they either have to be spiritual giants or have tremendous spiritual insight before they are worthy enough to share. Both of these perspectives are inaccurate and defeating. First of all, there are few, if any, true spiritual giants. We may think of some as being spiritual superheroes, but in reality no one has more direct access to God than you do. No one is "special." We are all subject to pitfalls and struggles. Give yourself a break. If you are waiting until you achieve sainthood, you may never share who you are.

Similarly, if you are waiting until you have some new and tremendous spiritual insight, you may also have a long wait. Solomon said, "There is nothing new under the sun" (Ecclesiastes 1:9). That's a fairly accurate statement, especially when it comes to spiritual insights. Any spiritual discovery that you make for yourself is actually a rediscovery. Someone else, somewhere else, has already discovered it.

This is basically true for all our spiritual discoveries, but that's okay. The importance of spiritual discoveries is not that they are new to the world but that they are new to us. We need to discover them for ourselves. It is in self-discovery that we "own" versus "borrow" our spiritual identity. Religion becomes real. Personal spiritual insights, no matter how insignificant they may appear, are worth sharing because they are real to you.

But even these rediscoveries will not occur every day. Growth is a slow and arduous process. So do not feel that you have little to offer just because there is nothing new in your life. Share how you *feel*. "I feel distant; I feel close; I feel blessed; I feel confused." Whatever you feel is fine, because that's what is real for you. How are you affected by what is happening in your life? That is important.

As Christians, we always have something to share because we are always in transit. We are always feeling, acting, and growing. Sometimes we are feeling up, sometimes down. Sometimes we are doing a lot, at other times very little. Sometimes we think we are growing by leaps and bounds, with many new personal insights and discoveries, while at other times we fail to see any movement at all. But wherever we are, we have something to share because of who we are, and relationships become more intimate when mates share who they are.

You and your mate may be at different places in your personal spiritual development, but that's okay   Jan and I are very different when it comes to our spirituality. This difference is the result of many factors, not just one. We have an entirely different heritage, our personalities are different, and the number of years that we have each spent walking with the Lord is different. Overall, much that contributes to who we are spiritually is quite dissimilar. I would guess that much the same could be said of you and your situation.

Sometimes who we are by nature causes us to make things more difficult than they have to be. Look at our situation, for example. Jan was raised in a stable Christian home, whereas my childhood environment was unstable and unchristian. Her natural outlook is trusting, whereas mine is "let me prove it first." She is a Peter, whereas I am a Thomas. Now, all of this is perfectly okay. Remember, these are differences, not deviances. But they are differences that affect how our spirituality develops.

Based on who Jan naturally is, things of faith have always come easier to her than to me. She is open and accepting; I have to evaluate. We Thomases grow—we just do so at a slower pace than some others might. One positive thing to be said of Thomases, however, is that the ground they cover is theirs. They may be slow, but they are sure. What they discover for themselves, in their own arduous and methodical manner, becomes a firm foundation. There is definitely nothing borrowed from another's faith; everything is owned.

The point that I am trying to make is this: There are a great many differences that operate in the spiritual lives of mates. In fact, there is far greater likelihood that any two mates will be at different places in their personal spiritual development than there is that they will be at the same. This being the case, be careful that you do not find yourself in the inferiority/superiority trap. Mates who see themselves at a different place spiritually from their partners sometimes view themselves as inferior. This feeling of spiritual inferiority commonly results in a hesitancy to share.

It may be true that you are not equal in spiritual insight.

There is a spiritual depth that only comes from maturity in the Lord. There is no shortcut to maturity; it requires time and experience, and even then, sometimes our personalities interfere with this process. Even though you may not be equal in insight, you are equal in opportunity to share your spiritual experience. There is equal opportunity to share what is real to you at this particular place in your own personal spiritual journey, and it is okay for you to be right where you are.

Mates are typically at different places spiritually, but this is not an indication of inferiority or a sign of superiority. It is merely an indication of reality. Do not let it be an interference to your sharing together.

What is sometimes thought of as spiritual "unworthiness" is actually an issue of spiritual "keenness" All of the respondents to the questionnaire were Christian. As I have already stated, for a Christian, the statement, "I'm not spiritual enough to share" is automatically negated. For Christians, right where they are is "shareable." It is authentic, it is real, and therefore, it is legitimate.

Furthermore, it is the normal flow of life to have some ups and downs. We do not always feel on top of the world or beneath it. Rather, there is an ebb and flow to our existence.

Be this as it may, sometimes the spiritual down times—the sense of being distant from the Lord, when there isn't much happening in our lives—are more the product of what we are doing than the natural ebb and flow of humanity. These times are usually the result of a faulty devotional life. The sense of being out of touch with the Lord may prompt a feeling of spiritual unworthiness and a hesitancy to share.

When this is the case, the solution is simple—it's just not easy. All that is needed is a personal spiritual growth plan and the discipline to follow through on it. The plan, modeled to your own requirements, will enable you to spend consistent time both in the Word and in prayer. The solution to your problem will come as you put action and discipline to your plan.

Developing a relationship with the Lord is no different from developing a relationship with a friend or loved one. You have to invest in it if it's going to happen. It requires that you *do* something.

My love for Jan is not something that I have to work up. I do not have to talk to myself, trying to psych myself up or trying to get some high emotional fervor going. It is a natural feeling. But even though my love for Jan is not something that I have to work up, it is something that I have to work at. I work *at* love for Jan by investing in our marriage. I give her my time, not just superficially but also in depth. I work at keeping blockages from coming between us. I do this by dealing with anger, by communicating directly instead of avoiding, and by being emotionally honest instead of dishonest. And I work at love for Jan by sharing myself with her emotionally, intellectually, and spiritually. What are the results of this investment? An intimate and bonded relationship.

Your relationship with the Lord develops in much the same manner. You cannot expect to feel connected and in relationship if you are not making concerted efforts to develop a personal spiritual relationship. The result of personal inactivity will be a lack of spiritual keenness, whereas the result of working *at* love with the Lord will be an enriched relationship. Once again, the solution is simple—it's just not always easy. It will require discipline and effort on your part. But the benefits are tremendous.

Start by remembering where you "lost your edge." Repent of your departure and ask the Lord's help as you commit to "seek first the Kingdom." Then develop a modest and accomplishable plan, something that will both meet your needs for growth and fit your schedule. Consistency is the key. As with the development of your conjoint plan for intimacy building, there are no right or wrong methods. You determine what will work best for you. You may even want to enlist the aid of your mate for accountability purposes or for running interference with children or others as you establish your own private time.

If spiritual keenness is a problem, it is at least a problem you can do something about, so do not let it interfere with your having a more spiritually intimate marriage. You can take charge of your life.

Final Thoughts

"I'm not spiritual enough to share." To say this is not a problem would be to deny reality. Many identify this as a definite interference to their achieving a more spiritually intimate marriage. But it is actually a problem of *attitude*, not one of spirituality. You are always spiritual enough to share. There are no spiritual giants here, no heroes. There's just you and me, clipping along at our own pace on our own spiritual journeys. At whatever point you may find yourself in this pilgrimage, that is real for you, and there is legitimacy in authenticity.

You may be different from your mate—different in heritage, personality, and experience. But that's okay. This makes you neither inferior nor superior. Rather, it makes you equal—equal in your worthiness before the Lord and equal in your opportunity to share what is real to you. By so doing, you will enhance your marriage.

Task

Your task this time is simple and unstructured. I want the two of you to talk about the problem of spiritual inferiority and whether it has played a role in your marriage. How are you different in your spiritual walks? Is one of you more accepting while the other is more evaluative? Does one of you seem to be further along in his or her spiritual pilgrimage? If so, do you let this interfere in your sharing?

Talk about how you view each other's spirituality and how that makes you feel about your own. Resolve any feelings of inferiority and superiority. Come away as equals.

12

"Our Spiritual Differences Are Divisive"

One of the prerequisites to spiritual intimacy is for you to have similar beliefs about God and religion. Yet, you can have similar beliefs and they still will not be identical. The fact that there will be some differences can be problematic.

The problem of nonidenticalness seems to be at the root of this statement:

> I think my mate does not accept my spirituality and does not allow me to be who I am. He/she is critical.

Special attention is focused on the terms describing nonaccepting and critical attitudes and behaviors. Obviously, attitudes and behaviors of this type interfere with the development of spiritual intimacy.

As was the case with feeling spiritually unworthy, a distinction must be drawn between beliefs that are deviant and those that are merely different. When it comes to the variant beliefs that exist within Christendom, there are a few of these that really matter, but there are a host of others that can be considered nonessential.

I was recently invited to be a counseling referral source for one of the many Christian organizations that receive calls from across the nation in search of such services. As part of the invitation, I had to complete a questionnaire that asked questions about my professional training and my religious beliefs and experience. All of this was aimed at determining my suitability as an approved referral source for this organization. Legitimately, this organization needed to have some degree of confidence in me before it would feel comfortable referring callers in my area for help. What I found amusing was the section entitled Doctrinal Description.

This section began with questions I considered essential. For example:

- Do you believe in the Scriptures as the authoritative Word of God?
- Do you believe in the threefold nature of God (Trinity), one in essence but separate in Person and distinct in duty?
- Do you believe that Christ is fully God and fully human and has completely satisfied sin's penalty by shedding His blood in dying for all mankind?

These questions, and a few of the others, were essential tenets of a Christian's faith. There is not much room for deviation. In fact, to disagree with these would probably be considered inconsistent with conservative evangelical thought. It would border on deviancy and account for more than just a difference in opinion. Yet, as the questionnaire continued, it moved further and further from Christian essentials to a point I considered extremely less than essential:

> Would you categorize your doctrine of last things as: premillennial, amillennial, or postmillennial?

My initial response was, "Who cares?" But the professional within me changed that response to a more acceptable, "No position taken."

I realize that these are three different positions regarding the end of time, and depending upon which of these you accept, different things are expected to occur. But really, how essential is your belief regarding the end of time to your present Christian experience and daily Christian walk?

Within the Christian context in which I most frequently find myself, it is the lesser essentials of Christian faith, and not the major tenets, that create the majority of the friction, and I believe this is totally uncalled for. When you get right down to it, there are few beliefs that are truly essential. With these less-essential areas, differences of opinion need to be considered as differences, not deviances. In these less-essential areas, liberty and acceptance, as opposed to rigidity, need to be our response.

Typical Differences

Do not misunderstand me. Less-essential areas can be important; they're just not more important than your relationship. When all is said and done, is the issue that seems to be dividing you really worth all the fuss? Probably not.

Most less-essential issues will fall into one of three categories. A brief description of these categories may aid your identification of the issues that present your difficulty.

Beliefs about "oughts" or "What we should be doing"
Our beliefs come from many different sources. Some we are taught in childhood, others we are taught as adults, and still

others we acquired on our own. It is important to understand why you believe what you believe. You may be holding on to a belief for all the wrong reasons. Or, even if the reasoning is good for you, it may not be totally applicable for your mate.

Church attendance is one of the oughts that I frequently hear complaints about. Friction does not generally emanate from Sunday-morning attendance. That is standard worship practice for most Christians. Differences of opinion, however, tend to arise around Sunday-evening and midweek activities. Some believe that church attendance is an indication of spirituality. From this perspective, truly devout people will be in church services whenever they are available. This belief is especially strong among those who were raised with this kind of expectation—third-, fourth-, and fifth-generation Christians. They may even feel guilty when a service is missed. Contrast this belief to a perspective that does not ascribe any particular spiritual connotation to church attendance. Which of these contrasting perspectives is right and which is wrong? Probably neither one. This is one of those less-essential areas.

What is important when these different positions are represented in a marriage is how this issue gets resolved. Will the decision be that both partners shall go to church on Sunday night and both are agreeable to this? Or will it be that they both go, but one is doing so under duress, his spirituality called into question if he fails to attend? Is the decision that they both stay at home, with both in agreement? Or is it that they both stay at home with the more traditional of the two feeling personal guilt for not being in church and harboring resentment for the one standing in his way? Will one go and one stay? This seems like an amiable solution unless the one who attends church makes moralizing statements to the one who chooses to remain at home. The options seem plentiful, but so are the opportunities for friction.

Other issues that easily fall into the "oughts" category would be beliefs regarding tithing and family devotions. Is the tithe 10 percent? Does it have to be given to the church that you attend, or can you earmark it for other ministries? Are there spiritual consequences for failing to tithe? How are family devotions handled? How frequently and when—daily? weekly? mornings? before bed?

Again, these are important issues in the life of a Christian family, but they are less than essential. What is of greatest importance is how they get resolved and what connotative meaning you attach to differing views. Do you despiritualize those who do not share your viewpoint? If so, the results of this kind of attitude may be more far-reaching than the issues themselves.

Beliefs about theology Theological beliefs can be too numerous to mention. I will suggest a few as examples, but in no way will this list exhaust the number of possible less-essential beliefs frequently endorsed by Christians.

It is necessary to note that these theological beliefs, though less essential than others, are still important. All of us as believers need to resolve these issues for ourselves. However, difficulty generally arises when, once a position is determined, it behooves one mate to convince his or her partner that this answer is *the* answer as opposed to *an* answer.

We are talking about less-essential issues. It is important that decisions be made regarding them, but these decisions need to be made on an independent basis. You can offer your opinion on what you have found to be true for you, but everyone has to discover his own answer, and generally this is *an* answer as opposed to *the* answer.

I have already mentioned the theological difference concerning the end of time, whether you choose to be a premil-

lennialist, an amillennialist, or a postmillennialist. A related
and popular issue would be whether we are presently living in
the last days. The fervor around the end of time seems to run
in cycles. Do you remember when some thought Henry Kis-
singer might possibly be the Antichrist? That was during my
college days, when Hal Lindsey's *The Late Great Planet Earth*
sparked renewed interest in the topic. Nearly twenty years
later, *88 Reasons for Christ's Return in 88* gained national attention, and we once again asked the question, "Are we living
in the last days?"

What's your position? I think this is an important issue, but
I do not think it is essential, and I definitely do not think it
should be divisive.

There are many issues that form and divide entire denom-
inations, but do not let them act divisively in your marriage.
They are important, but they are not essential. Answer these
questions for yourself and share what you discover with your
mate, but do not despiritualize him or her for failing to find
the same answer. Allow your spouse the freedom to develop
as you have.

Beliefs about the nature of God   It is not unusual to find
mates having differing views of the nature of God and the
process of spiritual development. The most frequent contrasts
are those between a view of God as righteous (just and disci-
plining) and one of Him as loving (nurturing and forgiving).
Actually, God is a blend of these, and that is generally the
belief held by both mates. It is seldom seen as an issue of
either/or, so we are not talking about a belief that necessarily
eliminates one of these two characteristics. Rather, we are
speaking of emphasis. There tends to be a leaning in one
direction or the other.

This nature-of-God category plays itself out around issues like growth process, relationship development between God and man, and God's view of our humanity. For example, a mate who leans toward a viewpoint emphasizing God's righteousness has more difficulty with human imperfection than does one who leans toward God as a loving and nurturing Father. Whereas one may feel guilty regarding noticeable imperfections, the other, though recognizing the same imperfections, has more of a sense of loving acceptance for who he is. He views himself as a creature en route to greater perfection, a journey that will require some time. He has some normal human frailties, but these will be refined. He views God as cutting him more slack than does his mate.

One mate might place more emphasis upon crisis religious experiences, whereas another might focus on the developmental process following these experiences. One might view the God-man relationship as forceful and powerful, whereas the other might view it as warmly intimate and loving.

Obviously all of these attributes are there. It's just that, largely because of who we are as individuals, we tend to focus on some aspects more than we do on others. What are the possible results to our marriages due to these differences? Sometimes varying views prompt divisiveness, but it need not be that way.

Dealing With Your Differences

There are going to be differences in your religious beliefs. These differences may be in the area of "oughts"; they may be more in theological issues; or they may be in how you view the nature of God. There could even be differences in all three of these categories. The fact that these differences exist is not only normal, it is also legitimate. It is impossible for any two people to be totally identical in their belief systems. What is important is not that differences exist but how they are handled. Are they constructively dealt with or are they allowed to be divisive?

Differences become divisive when we either fail to deal with them directly (thus creating blockage in the relationship) or despiritualize the differing mate. In an effort to forestall the divisiveness that can come from spiritual differences, I would encourage you to deal with them healthily. To do so, the following suggestions may prove helpful.

Recognize the issue   Clear identification is essential. What exactly is the difference that is creating the friction? Do not function in denial. This is not something that needs to be avoided. Rather, it is something that needs to be handled.

Affirm that it will not divide the two of you   The difference exists, but that is okay. Differences are legitimate. Affirm to each other the supremacy of your relationship over any difference that may exist. "You can be who you are, and that's okay."

Let God have the job of helping you grow   We get into trouble when we think that our mate has to see things the way we do. We think, "If he were just open to the leadership of the Lord, he would change." Maybe this observation is correct, and someday maybe he will change. But if this is the case, let the Lord do the changing.

We *are* changeable, and God is not beyond helping us grow from where we currently find ourselves, but we need to let Him do the job. To cross your mate's boundaries is to interfere with his development. It only prompts reaction, not closeness.

Choose to deal with it directly Avoiding the subject, pulling back when it is brought up, and hit-and-run tactics are all examples of failing to deal directly with a problem. These tactics result in nonresolution and blockage of a relationship. If you want to move toward some form of resolution regarding the differences that prevent closeness in your relationship, you need to deal with them directly.

There are a number of constructive means from which to choose for dealing with problems. Here are a few options available to you. The important thing is that you *both choose* to deal directly with the interference.

Choose to talk about it now. The goal of facing the issue and talking about it is not necessarily that one or both of you will change. Neither is it that, after one encounter, all of the feelings around the issue will be resolved. That would be nice, but it may not happen. Rather, you are beginning a process toward resolution. You are being heard.

In your discussion, talk about how you *feel*. Determine why you feel the way you do. Identify where your beliefs are rooted. Where do they come from? In comparison with everything else that is meaningful to you, how much real importance do you place on this difference of opinion?

Opening a dialogue like this can help soften positions held on both sides of an issue. Understanding why there is significance is important. But again, it is equally important that we do not demand that others necessarily place the same degree of significance on less-essential issues that we have grown to do. Respecting each other's right to be a separate individual is healthy and constructive for the development of a relationship.

Choose to prepare for a later discussion. Possibly you are not prepared to discuss the issue now. You may not be emotionally up to it, or the time is not right, or you need to collect your thoughts. Whatever the rationale, now is not a good time. But you do want to deal directly with the issue that blocks closeness in your relationship, so what do you do? Make a date!

By setting a time and place in the future when the two of you will come together for the specific purpose of talking about your particular interference, you are choosing to deal with your problem. You are making the statement, "We will not avoid this any longer." In so doing, it is important to set a time that is mutually agreeable and imperative that the appointment be kept. Commit to each other that no one will be stood up.

Choose to call a time-out if your discussion becomes heated. You may have chosen to have a cool, calm, and collected discussion regarding a difference that exists in your relationship, but somewhere in the process, emotions got heated. What do you do? Let the discussion deteriorate? Move to a full-blown argument? Instead, call a time-out.

Time-outs need to be used sparingly and not abused. You do not opt to stop a conversation at the first sign of disagreement or display of emotion. We are emotional beings; we need to be able to deal with them. But if emotions are running so strong that the clarity of focus has been lost or the discussion has degenerated to attacks and rebuffs, it is time to stop the spiraling decline. Call a time-out.

Time-outs work best with prearrangement. You establish a standing rule that, during any discussion, if either one of you feels the conversation is deteriorating, a time-out can be called. Whenever this is done, the other mate commits to honor it. However, another part of this prearranged agreement is a time frame whereby the discussion will be resumed.

The goal of a time-out is not to end a discussion, just to delay it. It is postponed to an agreed-upon later time. With the interruption, it is hoped that cooler minds will prevail in the renewed discussion.

Choose to not deal with it. This may appear to be a funny way of dealing with a problem area. Obviously, it will not do much to facilitate any compromises in what you may be doing, but it does seem to bring some reduction in tension.

In essence, you are choosing to bring the problem out into the open. Rather than reactively drawing back, denying, or avoiding it by some other means, you are declaring, "There is a problem here, but we are not yet ready to deal with it." You are choosing to place the issue on the back shelf for the time being, with the full intent of dealing with it at some later, unspecified, more appropriate time.

Care must be taken that this strategy does not become license. You cannot apply it to every issue. That would be abuse. Even with those issues where it is used, ultimately the issue will need to be faced. This approach needs to be viewed in the same manner as our federal income taxes. There is an automatic extension available to all citizens, but eventually everyone has to file.

Final Thoughts

No matter how similar your religious beliefs may be, there are going to be differences in how you see things. The root of these differences may be personality, heritage, or your own personal experiences. Jan was raised in a Christian environment in rural Alabama, the Bible Belt of the nation. I was raised in a nonchristian home in metropolitan Southern California. Obviously, we each have differing views on some issues. But these are lesser issues, not the essential ones.

Differences are bound to exist, but that is not the significant factor. What is important is how you deal with these differences of opinion. Do you avoid them, thus allowing them to be blockages in your relationship? Do you despiritualize your mate for not believing the way you do? Both of these responses are counterproductive to the development of a more spiritually intimate relationship.

Differences need to be faced—and they need to be faced healthily. As you deal directly with these issues, you will find that you can deal with something as sensitive as religious differences and not perish. Differing perspectives can be resolved.

Jan has contrasted to me on several occasions what she believes to be the difference between insight and growth. Insight is fast—growth is slow. Insight is fun—growth is work. As you begin to deal directly with each other, I believe you will find this to be true for you. There will be insight and there will be growth, but neither will come without time and work.

Finally, be accepting and nonjudgmental. If your mate becomes vulnerable enough to share how he or she really feels about something, do not be ridiculing or rejecting. That would constitute a true hurt. A lot of time is required for wounds of this nature to heal. Rather, accept and affirm his or her sharing. You do not have to agree with his or her position, but you do need to accept his right to have it.

Task

No matter how similar we may be in our spiritual beliefs and experiences, we are not totally alike. There are always some differences. Sometimes these differences can create enough tension or discomfort to act as a blockage in our drawing closer together spiritually.

In an effort to prevent differences from interfering with your developing a greater level of spiritual intimacy, the first part of your task is to make a list of the ways you believe you differ from your mate in spiritual areas. Do this separately. Cite how you feel and believe and how your mate feels and believes, thus demonstrating the differences. The difference may be in the area of beliefs about what Christians ought to be doing, theological issues, or your particular beliefs about the nature of God. Whatever these spiritual differences may be, it is best to acknowledge them as opposed to denying and avoiding them.

After compiling your lists, exchange, read, and think through your mate's observations. Do you agree or disagree? Do you have a clearer understanding of the differences?

Finally, discuss your findings. Establish a context of healthy communication as opposed to avoidance.

This entire exercise is meant for clarification and acceptance. You may find that there are fewer differences than you thought. On the other hand, you may find that there are more. Regardless, accept the position in your relationship that "you can be who you are. That's okay with me." These are Christian less essentials; you can allow some liberty here.

End the task by affirming your love for each other and your renewed commitment to pursuing a relationship marked by greater spiritual intimacy. Differences do not have to hinder your togetherness.

13
"We Don't Have the Time"

I was conducting a seminar on spiritual intimacy and opened one of the sessions with the question, "What stops you from sharing your spiritual journey with each other?" There were numerous responses, largely dealing with the interferences I have already discussed. Then a few of the participants began to talk about the problem of not having enough time to be spiritually intimate.

As they continued to speak, others in the group began nodding their heads as if to offer support for what they were hearing. There seemed to be a lot of identification with the complaints being voiced. After the responses slowed down, I affirmed their concerns regarding the problem of time. I also suggested that lack of time might not be quite the problem they thought it was.

It's not unusual, at the end of a seminar session, for a few of the participants to mingle and discuss what has just transpired. Sometimes they talk among themselves, sometimes they talk to me, and sometimes they do both. This night was no exception. After a few minutes of conversation, the minglers began to gradually disperse. As I began to gather my materials, I looked up to find that one participant remained behind. Her name was Betty.

This particular seminar was scheduled to meet every Tuesday evening for six consecutive weeks. Betty had been faithful in both attendance and participation. Her husband, Doug, had been to some of the sessions. However, his work schedule required him to do some traveling. This limited his ability to consistently attend any activity that extended beyond two or three weeks.

Betty was one of those people whom you naturally enjoy being around. She possessed a pleasant, cheerful demeanor, and her comments were always helpful and positive. Although not exceptionally outgoing, neither was she shy and retiring. Betty had expressive eyes that projected warmth and calmness. In short, she seemed to strike a comfortable balance in many of her characteristics, immediately placing those around her at ease.

This description of Betty had been accurate throughout the the seminar, but it did not fit the woman who now stood before me. This person was troubled. Betty's brow was furrowed, and her jaw was tight. Her eyes continued to be expressive, but now they were intense and penetrating. Perplexed, confused, frustrated—possibly one of these terms would be appropriate for Betty. I didn't know yet, but if I could read faces at all, "pleasant and calm" were definitely out. Betty began to speak, and what follows is an abbreviated account of the dialogue that ensued.

Betty: Some of the things that were discussed tonight are confusing for me. I was wondering if we could talk about them.

Dr. Harvey: Sure, Betty. I've got some time. What was it that confused you?

Betty: When the group was discussing how time can be a real problem, you said that it may not be the problem we think it is. What did you mean by that?

Dr. Harvey: I think that not having enough time is a problem we all face and, to some extent, it limits the degree to which we do anything productive, including working on the spiritual aspect of our marriages. But if we are doing nothing in regard to developing spiritual intimacy in our relationship, it's probably *not* solely a time issue.

Betty: I don't know if I totally understand what you are saying. In my own situation, for instance, Doug and I simply don't have the time to share together. This isn't the kind of thing that can be done anytime, anywhere. We would need some prime quality time and some privacy. Both of these are in short supply in our home.

Dr. Harvey: Why is that? What are the demands on your schedule? What makes life so hectic for you and Doug?

Betty: Doug's job is demanding. It's not unusual for him to be out of town one or two nights a week. And even when he is in town, he's not usually on a convenient eight-to-five schedule. We've got three school-age children to get to-and-fro, and one of them is a teenager. The entire family is active in church. I'm thankful for a church that has so much to offer its members, but with the normal services, special programs for Doug and me, and the youth activities, we seem to be constantly on the go. Does that answer your question?

Dr. Harvey: You and Doug certainly do sound busy. With that kind of schedule, about how often do you find time to share and pray together?

Betty: Never. I'm really embarrassed to say it, but we simply do not have the time—ever.

Dr. Harvey: I'm curious, Betty. What else do you *not* have the time to do?

Betty: What do you mean?

Dr. Harvey: You said that you and Doug never have the opportunity to be spiritually intimate, that the time just isn't there. Are there other things that you never do?

Betty: Well, I don't know. I'm not sure. I can't really think of any right off the top of my head.

Dr. Harvey: What about social things like getting together with friends or going to parties? Do you ever do these things?

Betty: Yes. We do them some.

Dr. Harvey: What about family things like spending time with your children or visiting relatives or taking vacations? Do you ever do these things?

Betty: Yes. We do them, too.

Dr. Harvey: What about marital things like going out to dinner with Doug or spending some romantic time together?

Betty: Yes. We occasionally have some time together—romantically and just the two of us.

Dr. Harvey: Now, you probably don't have the opportunity to do these as much as you would like. Do you?

Betty: No, we don't.

Dr. Harvey: But you do do them some.

Betty: Yes.

Dr. Harvey: So, in the midst of a busy and hectic life-style, you and Doug have time to do these things some, but are never spiritually intimate.

Betty: Yeah. I think I'm beginning to understand.

Dr. Harvey: There's nothing wrong with any of these activities, Betty. I do them all, too. And, like you, I'd like to do some of them more often. But of one thing you can be certain: If I like or want to do anything at all, I will at least do it some.

Betty: Okay. I see what you're saying. Maybe Doug and I need to look at our situation again.

This dialogue with Betty was not surprising. Nor was it unusual. After all, lack of time received a third-place ranking overall as an interference, according to questionnaire respondents. Yet, I question how truly legitimate time problems can be.

In *The Drifting Marriage*, I devoted an entire chapter to the issue of "hecticness" and how our life-styles can unsuspectingly interfere with the development of intimacy in our marriages. Worthy causes and enrichment activities can choke the life out of a relationship. But to say that hecticness prevents us from ever sharing together spiritually may very well be a deception on our part.

There are many legitimate activities that compete for your time. But even without a plan of action that intentionally focuses your attention on the development of spiritual intimacy in your marriage, the competition for time would not account for questionnaire responses of "almost never."

I have heard it said that we always find time to do what we want to do. I'm not so idealistic as to believe this statement. At least, I'm not so idealistic as to believe that we always find time to do what we want to do as much as we would like to do it. But I am idealistic enough to think that when we want to, we do better than almost never.

Possibly, you don't get to share together as much as you would like. On a scale of 1 to 10, you are a 5. But time is not *the* problem if you are a 1. Time can be a problem, but it's not nearly as significant as you would like to believe.

What You Can Do

If not having time is your problem, whether it is not having enough time, the right time, or any time, it's time that you faced reality. It is unlikely that time is really your problem. I'm not exactly sure what your real problem is. But of one thing I am fairly certain: it isn't time.

There needs to be a thorough reassessment of why you do what you do. Take another look at the Spiritual Intimacy in Marriage Questionnaire. If there is an interference on that list that would be your second choice, what would it be? That is probably the true interference in your relationship.

Change comes with facing reality and assuming responsibility for what you find. Reality in this instance is that time isn't your problem—something else is. It may be personal discomfort with sharing. It may be that you have grown weary of sharing, only to find your self-disclosing nonreciprocated. It may be something all together different from anything suggested in this book. But the real question is this: Regardless of what the interference may be, what are you going to *do* about it? Are you going to assume responsibility for what you have found? And if so, exactly how are you going to do it?

Final Thoughts

You don't have the time? I disagree. In reality, you don't have the time not to invest in the spiritual aspect of your marriage. The benefits far outweigh the costs.

Facing reality is not always easy. It is far easier to continue in denial and convince yourself that the real problem is an issue of time constraints. But you know that is not the case.

Just as facing the reality of your true interference is difficult, so is taking responsibility for what you find. But it is only as you do both—discover and act—that change occurs. The choice is yours.

14
"How Do We Keep It Going?"

The final thought that seems to arise whenever I complete a spiritual intimacy seminar is this: "How do we keep it going?" One participant summed it up this way:

> We've had six weeks of sessions to keep us focused and dealing with each other. Without that structure, will we be disciplined enough to continue in our plan to be spiritually intimate? What could we do to keep it going?

This is a very legitimate concern and one probably based on experience. All of us have started projects that we fail to see completed. We have well-intended motivation at the outset, but somewhere along the way our worthy endeavor gets abandoned. It may be that other activities successfully competed for our time and the project was simply crowded out of our schedule. This can happen quite subtly. Or maybe it was a more obvious abandonment: after due consideration, the project was no longer considered a worthy goal. Whatever the reason, many projects, although begun with fervor, fail to be taken to completion. Is that the destiny of your efforts toward becoming more spiritually intimate?

If you want to keep it going—to continue in your quest for greater spiritual intimacy in your marriage—there are some specific things you can do. Likewise, there are some equally specific things that you should not do. This chapter will focus on these *do*s and *don't*s, with the goal that this quest will become a continuing part of your life-style.

How to Keep a Good Thing Going

These are the *do*s. If you want to continue in the direction of change and growth, these suggestions will aid you in your quest.

Hold the time sacred   This factor is especially important. Granted, there will always be occasions when unexpected or unavoidable interferences will arise. But these need to be held in check. If these interfering incidents become frequent, they take on the nature of a pattern, and interfering patterns are unacceptable.

Sometimes schedule restraints require that your designated time together be permanently changed. That's okay. There is nothing sacred about when you meet. What is important is that you meet. Do what works for you. If a permanent change needs to be made, fine; do what you need to do in order to ensure a time together.

At other times, an unavoidable responsibility will need to take priority over your sharing time. This is a temporary, not permanent, interruption. This will occasionally happen. It would be good for you to devise a plan for dealing with just such an occurrence. For example, one couple from a seminar reported that when they foresaw an event that would unavoidably interfere with their weekly time together, they would set an alternative time to meet that would precede their regular time. This guarded against the possibility of their time together getting lost in the shuffle.

Whether or not you develop a method as elaborate as this, of one thing be certain: many worthy activities will vie for your time together. To maintain your progress will require that you firmly hold to your designated time.

Deal with some content that you have in common Your goal is not to place yourself in a situation where you feel as though you have to produce. To eliminate this performance anxiety, it is helpful to have some content (written material) that you can share. This can be the Bible, study aids, or inspirational books. Utilizing written material allows you to share yourself less directly. You do this by concentrating on the content being considered.

- What does this material mean to me?
- How does it make me feel?
- Do I agree or disagree with it?
- Can I identify with it?
- How does it speak to me?

These are the types of questions that allow sharing yet reduce the personal pressure often associated with self-disclosure.

Be flexible and creative regarding what you do with your time Do not feel restricted to a set format during your time together. You can vary your activity. Some options would be:

Take a walk. Some seminar couples call this the "walk and talk." Nowhere is it stated that you have to sit and talk. The change can be exhilarating.

Go out and celebrate. A quiet corner in a restaurant can be a refreshing change to meeting in your living room. Do this occasionally as a celebration of the changes being made in your marriage due to your time together.

Have a couple worship service. You may want to structure one of your times together as a worship service. If so, each of you could assume different responsibilities.

Be creative. There are many ways to vary your time together, and occasional changes in routine can prevent monotony from influencing an otherwise worthy endeavor.

Schedule a reevaluation   "Take your pulse" every two or three months. This needs to be a scheduled time to regularly allow for a reevaluation. Use this time for making necessary adjustments:

- Are we heading in the direction in which we want to go?
- Is progress being made?
- Are there interferences?
- Is there something we could be doing differently?
- Are we satisfied with the plan as is?

These types of questions are especially helpful as you check on your progress. Be objective, not critical. If things are not going as you would like, don't blame, adjust. This is a constructive time, not destructive. Work together to make your plan better.

Plan a spiritual retreat weekend   This needs to be done at least annually. Plan to get away for an entire weekend with the primary focus on dealing with each other spiritually.

Needless to say, do not take your children. This is a time for the two of you, not the family. Ideally, you will find a retreat facility to accommodate your weekend together, but that is not an essential requirement. Where is not as important as what. As long as you have some privacy and can maintain your focus, this can be a productive and enriching time.

Maintain appropriate and realistic expectations You will want to remember two things:

Change is gradual. Do not expect instantaneous change. True change occurs gradually over time. Growth is a process, not an event, so do not set yourself up for needless frustration by having unrealistic expectations.

Intimate relationships are the result of planning. Intimate experiences can occur spontaneously. But intimate relationships are the result of planning. They do not just happen; they require effort.

How to Prevent a Good Thing From Happening

These are the *don't*s. If you want to interfere with the progress that has been made in your relationship, these are the activities that will do it. Therefore, avoid these at all costs.

Let your time together get too heavy There will be times of intensity—times when emotions peak and the things being shared are burdensome. That is to be expected. But there must be a balance maintained in your time together. To be totally heavy is to be too heavy.

Your time together needs to also be uplifting and esteeming. This is accomplished by sharing positives as opposed to just negatives; by discussing lighter subjects in addition to the heavier issues; and by utilizing content, thereby having the opportunity to share indirectly, as opposed to keeping the focus directly on yourself.

If your time together is always heavy and intense, it will become dreaded. Maintain a healthy balance so the changes you are making can be continued.

Fall into old patterns   Being critical and judgmental about differing beliefs; defensively withdrawing or attacking when your feelings are hurt; avoiding discussion because of anticipated rejection—these are the kind of interpersonal patterns that prevented your closeness in the past. If you want to prevent closeness in the future, just pick these patterns back up. Your progress will be stopped dead in its tracks.

You will find that it is easy to slip back into old patterns. After all, they were such a part of your life for so long. But now, at least with healthier couples, it's harder to stay in them. You know too much. Before, these destructive habits were enacted without much thought. Your response was automatic. The patterns were largely unrecognized—they were covert. Now, they are visible. To continue in them means to do so with intent, and most of us are not willing to intentionally move in a nonconstructive direction.

Watch for the old patterns. Point them out to each other if you see them. This is one instance where the better you know the rules, the harder it is to play the game.

Allow the focus to move from things of a spiritual nature
Remember what this time together is and what it is not. It is *not:*

- a time to discuss running the household
- a time to discuss children
- a time for catching up with what has been going on (other than what pertains to you spiritually)
- a time to discuss only grievances
- a time to talk church
- a time to discuss only theology

* a marital counseling session: "This is what's wrong with our marriage"

This *is* a time to focus on your spiritual lives together, to share and have this sharing reciprocated.

Have excessive expectations I have already mentioned that change is slow and gradual. Viewing it, therefore, as something that should occur instantaneously would be unreasonable. Also unreasonable would be the expectation that every time you meet together will be a spiritual high. That is simply not the case.

As there are highs and lows in most areas of life, these times of sharing together will be no different. There will be dry times and there will be overflowing times. Be thankful for both. As you remain faithful to your commitment to each other, your marriage will grow.

How to Deal With Backsliding

Backsliding is one of those terms that sparks a varied set of emotions when used in a theological context. Quite frankly, that is the least of my intentions; I am not trying to use the word in a theological sense. Yet, I can think of no better phrase to describe what occasionally occurs between marriage partners who set out to become more spiritually intimate. Sometimes they backslide.

When this occurs, what do you do? Quit? Start over? Pick up where you left off? There seem to be a lot of options. Let me offer some suggestions.

Recognize that it will probably happen At some time, whether in your relationship or mine, the chances are likely that we will backslide in our commitment to work toward greater spiritual intimacy. It may be that we let other demands subtly rob us of our appointed time together. Or, less subtly, we may lapse into more comfortable patterns of non-self-disclosure.

Whatever the motivation, do not lose hope. Refrain from feeling like a failure. Sure, you messed up, but that's not the end of the world. Just deal with it.

Choose to deal with your backsliding in a restorative manner It is best to have a pre-agreed-upon plan of restoration, just in case you ever need one. The following steps may be helpful:

Commit to deal with backsliding. By prearrangement, agree to deal with any occurrence of backsliding that is brought to your attention. When you are made aware of the situation, do not continue in denial or avoidance.

Be objective. As much as possible, be objective and nonjudgmental. Focus on correcting the problem as opposed to blaming each other.

Assess and discuss what got you derailed. Learn from your mistakes. Was it discomfort? Was it poor prioritizing of events and time? Was it expectations that were too high and thus discouraging? Was it the lack of a good plan to start with?

What allowed you to derail from your committed destination of greater spiritual intimacy could have been any number of things. Determine exactly what it was. How did it happen? Who did what? The better you understand what it was and how it happened, the better you will be able to correct the problem and prevent a reccurrence.

Recommit to your goal and (new) plan. Getting back on track is easy. You just reaffirm your commitment to be spiritually intimate and begin implementing your structured plan of action. It may be that there was nothing wrong with the old plan, other than faithfulness in following it. On the other hand, possibly revisions are needed. Whichever the case, you get back on track by beginning again. You take action.

Backsliding is probably inevitable, but its occurrence does not have to mark the end of a journey. You can start again with renewed vigor to have all that God intends for your marriage.

Conclusions
Is It Worth the
Effort?

Spiritual intimacy—is it real? Is it achievable? If so, is it essential? These are difficult questions I have endeavored to answer throughout this book. What are my conclusions regarding these questions of spiritual intimacy?

- It is real but seldom recognized.
- It is achievable but seldom experienced.
- Although it is not essential, it is a blessed marriage that attains it.

In attempting to lay a foundation of understanding for spiritual intimacy, I have tried to differentiate between what it is and what it is not. In this regard, spiritual intimacy is not automatic. It does not come with the marriage license, the pronouncement of "I do," or the fact that you are both Christians. Nor is it easy. If spiritual intimacy is present at all, it is because you both desire it and are willing to pay the price to achieve it. Finally, it is not instantaneous. Spiritual intimacy does not just suddenly appear. It is gradual—the result of a process of growth.

What it is, however, is *intended*. Actually, there are many other descriptive terms that could be listed here, but I think this is the most essential. God always intends His children to have His best, and when it comes to realizing the true benefits of marriage, there is nothing more rewarding than spiritual closeness with your mate.

You are created for intimacy. This is the Master design. You can have all the other dimensions of closeness (emotional, intellectual, sexual, social, and recreational), but if you are lacking the spiritual, you are really missing out. Nothing else so enhances a marriage. Nothing else brings the warmth. And nothing else brings the strength. It is the essence of God's plan. Truly, God intends only the best for His children.

Is it real? Is it accomplishable? Is it essential? These are all good questions. But probably a better closing question is this: "Is it worth the effort?" This is a question that can only be answered individually. Personally, I can answer yes, for I have found it to be definitely worth the effort in my marriage. Jan and I have not yet arrived, but we are on our way, and because of this, I can offer the added encouragement that you experience it for yourself—that you "taste and find." But this is a decision you alone must make.

In closing, let me leave you with one final reminder: It is always worth the effort to "have all that God intends."

Appendix
Spiritual Intimacy in Marriage Questionnaires

Spiritual Intimacy in Marriage Questionnaire (husband's form)

The Spiritual Intimacy in Marriage Questionnaire is designed to gather information about the level of spiritual closeness that exists within a marriage. Some of the questions require information about yourself, whereas others seek your opinion of your wife. Although most of the questions relate directly to spiritual and religious issues within your marriage (what you do, think, feel), a few of them seek to gain information about your marriage in a more general sense. Regardless of the content, please try to answer all of the questions.

Thank you in advance for taking the time to complete this questionnaire. I appreciate your willingness to put forth the effort. You need not fear that someone will become aware of your answers. All of the questionnaires are totally anonymous. So please be honest in your responses. Your candid responses will be very helpful in aiding the understanding of this important area of marital life.

1. How long have you been in this marriage?
   _____ Less than 2 years
   _____ 2 to 5 years

_____ 6 to 10 years
_____ 11 to 15 years
_____ 16 to 25 years
_____ More than 25 years

2. As a whole, how satisfied are you with your marriage? (check appropriate answer)
_____ Very satisfied (there is little that needs changing)
_____ Fairly satisfied (there are a few things that need changing)
_____ Satisfied
_____ Fairly dissatisfied (there are a number of things that need changing)
_____ Very dissatisfied (many things need changing. My relationship is in real trouble)

3. How similar are your beliefs about God and religion as compared with those of your wife?
_____ Very similar
_____ Similar
_____ Different
_____ Very different

4. How important is your religious faith to you?
_____ Very important
_____ Somewhat important
_____ Not very important
_____ Of no importance

5. In your opinion, how important is your wife's religious faith to her?
_____ Very important
_____ Somewhat important
_____ Not very important
_____ Of no importance

6. Are you a Christian?
_____ Yes
_____ No
If yes, for how many years?

_____ Less than 2 years

_____ 2 to 5 years

_____ 6 to 10 years

_____ 11 to 15 years

_____ 16 to 25 years

_____ More than 25 years

7. To the best of your knowledge, is your wife a Christian?

_____ Yes

_____ No

If yes, for how many years? (if uncertain, select your best guess)

_____ Less than 2 years

_____ 2 to 5 years

_____ 6 to 10 years

_____ 11 to 15 years

_____ 16 to 25 years

_____ More than 25 years

8. How close do you feel to your wife spiritually?

_____ Very close

_____ Somewhat close

_____ Neutral

_____ Somewhat distant

_____ Very distant

9. How frequently do the two of you discuss religious and denominational news, i.e., what is happening at church; new church programs; what church friends are doing; "church talk"; etc.?

_____ Very frequently (nearly daily)

_____ Occasionally (weekly)

_____ Very infrequently (monthly)

_____ Almost never

10. How frequently do the two of you discuss with each other theological issues, i.e., beliefs about religion or doctrine, although not of a personal nature (superficial . . . not as it applies to what is happening in your own personal life)?

_____ Very frequently (nearly daily)

_____ Occasionally (weekly)

_____ Very infrequently (monthly)

_____ Almost never

11. How frequently do the two of you share with each other what is happening in your own spiritual lives, i.e., what God is doing for you personally (nonsuperficial sharing of personal growth, struggles, insights, etc.)?

_____ Very frequently (nearly daily)

_____ Occasionally (weekly)

_____ Very infrequently (monthly)

_____ Almost never

12. Which do you find to be the *easiest* (most comfortable) to talk about with your wife? (Rank your comfort with each by marking the easiest 1st, and so on. Mark *each* space.)

_____ Talking about religious and denominational news

_____ Talking about theological issues and religious beliefs

_____ Talking about personal spiritual growth, struggles, and insights

13. How frequently do you pray together (other than at mealtimes)?

_____ Very frequently (nearly daily)

_____ Occasionally (weekly)

_____ Very infrequently (monthly)

_____ Almost never

14. How satisfied are you with the frequency level of personal sharing about truly spiritual matters (question 11) that is taking place between you and your wife?

_____ Very satisfied

_____ Somewhat satisfied (okay but could be better)

_____ Somewhat dissatisfied (really could stand improvement)

_____ Very dissatisfied

15. If you were not able to answer "very satisfied" to question 14, what is it that prevents you from sharing personal spiritual matters with your wife? (Indicate every item that applies in order of significance, i.e., 1st, 2d, etc.)

_____ I find it too uncomfortable to share something that personal.

_____ My wife is not spiritual enough for me to share with.

_____ I'm not spiritual enough to share.

_____ I think my wife does not accept my spirituality and does not allow me to be who I am. She is critical.

_____ I get tired of sharing when my wife will not share with me.

_____ My wife is not interested in listening to what I have to share.

_____ I feel good about my personal spiritual relationship but do not see the need to share with my wife.

_____ Is there a reason not listed?_____

16. If you were not able to answer "very satisfied" in question 14, to the best of your knowledge, what is it that prevents your wife from sharing personal spiritual matters with you? (Indicate every item that applies in order of significance, i.e., 1st, 2d, etc.)

_____ My wife finds it too uncomfortable to share something that personal.

_____ My wife is not spiritual enough to share with me.

_____ My wife does not believe I am spiritual enough to share with.

_____ She thinks I do not accept her spirituality and do not allow her to be who she is. She feels I'm critical.

_____ My wife has tried to share with me but has grown tired of trying because I have not shared myself in return.

_____ My wife is spiritually sound but does not see the need to share with me.

_____ She thinks I am not interested in her sharing of spiritual concerns with me.

_____ Is there a reason not listed?_____

Spiritual Intimacy in Marriage Questionnaire (wife's form)

The Spiritual Intimacy in Marriage Questionnaire is designed to gather information about the level of spiritual closeness that exists within a marriage. Some of the questions require information about yourself, whereas others seek your opinion of your husband. Although most of the questions relate directly to spiritual and religious issues within your marriage (what you do, think, feel), a few of them seek to gain information about your marriage in a more general sense. Regardless of the content, please try to answer all of the questions.

Thank you in advance for taking the time to complete this questionnaire. I appreciate your willingness to put forth the effort. You need not fear that someone will become aware of your answers. All of the questionnaires are totally anonymous. So please be honest in your responses. Your candid responses will be very helpful in aiding the understanding of this important area of marital life.

1. How long have you been in this marriage?
   _____ Less than 2 years

_____ 2 to 5 years

_____ 6 to 10 years

_____ 11 to 15 years

_____ 16 to 25 years

_____ More than 25 years

2. As a whole, how satisfied are you with your marriage? (check appropriate answer)

_____ Very satisfied (there is little that needs changing)

_____ Fairly satisfied (there are a few things that need changing)

_____ Satisfied

_____ Fairly dissatisfied (there are a number of things that need changing)

_____ Very dissatisfied (many things need changing. My relationship is in real trouble)

3. How similar are your beliefs about God and religion as compared with those of your husband?

_____ Very similar

_____ Similar

_____ Different

_____ Very different

4. How important is your religious faith to you?

_____ Very important

_____ Somewhat important

_____ Not very important

_____ Of no importance

5. In your opinion, how important is your husband's religious faith to him?

_____ Very important

_____ Somewhat important

_____ Not very important

_____ Of no importance

6. Are you a Christian?

_____ Yes

_____ No

If yes, for how many years?

_____ Less than 2 years

_____ 2 to 5 years

_____ 6 to 10 years

_____ 11 to 15 years

_____ 16 to 25 years

_____ More than 25 years

7. To the best of your knowledge, is your husband a Christian?

_____ Yes

_____ No

If yes, for how many years? (if uncertain, select your best guess)

_____ Less than 2 years

_____ 2 to 5 years

_____ 6 to 10 years

_____ 11 to 15 years

_____ 16 to 25 years

_____ More than 25 years

8. How close do you feel to your husband spiritually?

_____ Very close

_____ Somewhat close

_____ Neutral

_____ Somewhat distant

_____ Very distant

9. How frequently do the two of you discuss religious and denominational news, i.e., what is happening at church; new church programs; what church friends are doing; "church talk"; etc.?

_____ Very frequently (nearly daily)

_____ Occasionally (weekly)

_____ Very infrequently (monthly)

_____ Almost never

10. How frequently do the two of you discuss with each other theological issues, i.e., beliefs about religion or doctrine, although not of a personal nature (superficial . . . not as it applies to what is happening in your own personal life)?

_____ Very frequently (nearly daily)
_____ Occasionally (weekly)
_____ Very infrequently (monthly)
_____ Almost never

11. How frequently do the two of you share with each other what is happening in your own spiritual lives, i.e., what God is doing for you personally (nonsuperficial sharing of personal growth, struggles, insights, etc.)?
_____ Very frequently (nearly daily)
_____ Occasionally (weekly)
_____ Very infrequently (monthly)
_____ Almost never

12. Which do you find to be the *easiest* (most comfortable) to talk about with your husband? (Rank your comfort with each by marking the easiest 1st, and so on. Mark *each* space.)
_____ Talking about religious and denominational news
_____ Talking about theological issues and religious beliefs
_____ Talking about personal spiritual growth, struggles, and insights

13. How frequently do you pray together (other than at mealtimes)?
_____ Very frequently (nearly daily)
_____ Occasionally (weekly)
_____ Very infrequently (monthly)
_____ Almost never

14. How satisfied are you with the frequency level of personal sharing about truly spiritual matters (question 11) that is taking place between you and your husband?
_____ Very satisfied
_____ Somewhat satisfied (okay but could be better)
_____ Somewhat dissatisfied (really could stand improvement)
_____ Very dissatisfied

15. If you were not able to answer "very satisfied" to question 14, what is it that prevents you from sharing personal spiritual matters with your husband? (Indicate every item that applies in order of significance, i.e., 1st, 2d, etc.)

_____ I find it too uncomfortable to share something that personal.

_____ My husband is not spiritual enough for me to share with.

_____ I'm not spiritual enough to share.

_____ I think my husband does not accept my spirituality and does not allow me to be who I am. He is critical.

_____ I get tired of sharing when my husband will not share with me.

_____ My husband is not interested in listening to what I have to share.

_____ I feel good about my personal spiritual relationship but do not see the need to share with my husband.

_____ Is there a reason not listed?_____

16. If you were not able to answer "very satisfied" to question 14, to the best of your knowledge, what is it that prevents your husband from sharing personal spiritual matters with you? (Indicate every item that applies in order of significance, i.e., 1st, 2d, etc.)

_____ My husband finds it too uncomfortable to share something that personal.

_____ My husband is not spiritual enough to share with me.

_____ My husband does not believe I am spiritual enough to share with.

_____ He thinks I do not accept his spirituality and do not allow him to be who he is. He feels I'm critical.

_____ My husband has tried to share with me but has grown tired of trying because I have not shared myself in return.

_____ My husband is spiritually sound but does not see the need to share with me.

_____ He thinks I am not interested in his sharing of spiritual concerns with me.

_____ Is there a reason not listed?_____

To the Reader

We welcome your thoughts, feelings, and reactions to the material presented in *The Spiritually Intimate Marriage*.

Correspondence and inquiries regarding speaking availability may be directed to Dr. Harvey at the following address:

Dr. Donald R. Harvey
P. O. Box 1128
Franklin, TN 37065

We cannot promise that Dr. Harvey will be able to respond to all letters he receives, but he will thoughtfully read every one. May God bless you in your journey toward spiritual intimacy.